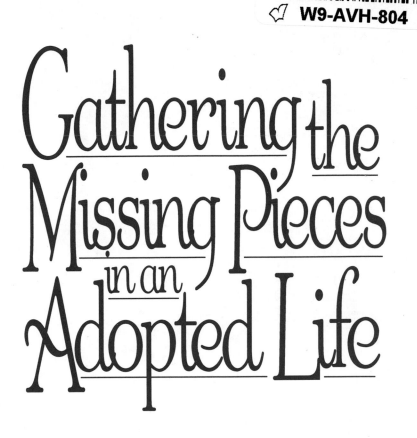

Gathering the Missing Pieces in an Adopted Life

Gathering the Missing Pieces in an Adopted Life

Kay Moore

BROADMAN
& HOLMAN
PUBLISHERS

Nashville, Tennessee

4253-55
0-8054-5355-5

Dewey Decimal Classification: 306.87
Subject Heading: Adopted Children / Adoptees
Library of Congress Card Catalog Number: 94-9667
Printed in the United States of America

Unless otherwise noted, all Scripture quotations are taken from the King James Version of the Bible.

Library of Congress Cataloging-in-Publication Data
Moore, Kay
  Gathering the missing pieces in an adopted life: completing your family album / by Kay Moore
      p. cm.
  Includes bibliographical references.
  ISBN 0-8054-5355-5
  1. Birth parents — United States — Identification. 2. Adoptees — United States — Psychology.
  I. Title
  HV875.55M66   1995
  362.82'98—dc20
                                          94-9667
                                            CIP

In memory of my father
J. D. Wheeler
1904-93

In honor of my mothers
Mable and Eleanor

In gratitude for those who walked through the fire,
Charles, Catharine, Louis, Matthew, and
Catharine Louisa

Dandelion Song

When you feel my step upon your soil, you may think it's a stranger's tread,

But I'll learn to sleep beneath your stars with your valleys for my bed.

For I'm your native daughter, tho' I had to be gone awhile.

I vowed one day I'd find you, if I had to walk ev'ry mile.

Say there, Colorado, won't you claim me now?

I've been gone so long, yet I had to get back somehow,

There's a long life still before me,

And I thank you for waiting for me,

Colorado, I've come back again.

My Colorado, I've come back again!

My feet were planted in a town that had no mountains high,

'Twas a good life, such a pleasant life, under that city sky.

But always deep inside me was a yearning back to roam.

And always dreaming of the day I'd find this mountain home.

Say there, Colorado, won't you claim me now?

I've been gone so long, yet I had to get back somehow,

There's a long life still before me,

And I thank you for waiting for me,

Colorado, I've come back again.

My Colorado, I've come back again!

I want to travel every road and see what's beyond the next hill,

Want to stand on every mountain peak and search out ev'ry thrill.

There's not enough hours in the day to pack all your glory in.

But I swear as I stand upon your soil, we'll not be parted again.

Say there, Colorado, won't you claim me now?

I've been gone so long, yet I had to get back somehow,

There's a long life still before me,

And I thank you for waiting for me,

Colorado, I've come back again.

My Colorado, I've come back again!

Contents

Foreword

🌿

*A*s a pastor I often was confronted with people involved in one of the various aspects of the adoption triad—families who want to adopt or who have adopted children; individuals who themselves were adopted, and people who find themselves contemplating whether to make an adoption plan for a child they cannot parent. I desperately needed to be able to recommend to them a resource such as Kay Moore's *Gathering the Missing Pieces in an Adopted Life: Completing Your Family Album.* I know of no other material that so thoroughly presents the practical, current issues surrounding adoption from such a compassionate, Christian perspective.

Many of us who hold to the sanctity of human life believe that Christians in the contemporary church must do all that we can to promote adoption as the best solution for women who feel they cannot rear their babies. This book is a positive, pro-life statement about how adoption can produce a Christ-honoring outcome for everyone affected. It even includes suggestions about what churches themselves can do to deal with these issues head-on to help support adoptive parents who struggle with child-rearing issues, to help adopted adults who wonder whether it is God's will for them to search for their birth family members, and to help birth parents who struggle with lonely, staggering decisions that will impact their lives for years to come.

By sharing her captivating personal story and how it has impacted her Christian witness—and by intertwining her adoption-related experiences with those of numerous other believers—Kay Moore rivets the reader while at the same time dispenses vast and valuable information on the nuts-and-bolts of every aspect of adoption. She presents an honest, frank, and realistic look at the lifelong challenges that families affected by adoption face. Yet, as this book contends, adoption has never been a better choice because of the lifeline of helps available to families today.

This landmark book should be required reading in every crisis pregnancy center, adoption agency, adoptive home, and church which has a burden to reach out and minister to people facing critical issues in their lives.

James T. Draper, Jr.
President, Baptist Sunday School Board
President, Southern Baptist Convention, 1982–84

Acknowledgments

*T*his *book could not have been written* without the help of numerous courageous adopted individuals, birth family members, adoptive parents, and persons involved helping all these groups who shared their struggles, heartaches, victories, and insights. To them goes a special thank-you for stepping outside the safe cocoon of privacy and volunteering details that might help another reader say, "That's how I felt, too! I never knew anyone that had that experience but me!"

Janis Whipple is an affirming editor at Broadman & Holman whose valor in the midst of a life-threatening illness has earned the admiration of many.

Keith Ninomiya's research into current adoption trends was valuable in helping tie my story to today's state-of-the-art practices.

I am deeply indebted to the management of the *Houston Chronicle* for taking seriously a newspaper's charge to raise the consciousness level of the community and therefore encouraging my writing of the series on adoption which serves as the basis for this narrative. Special thanks to managing editors Don Pickels and Tony Pederson for supporting me in a community-service role as the public responded during the months and years of its aftermath, and to Lifestyle Editor Beverly Harris for her sensitive editing and shaping of the "Dandelion" project.

The Beginning:
An Unusual Kind of Homecoming

※

I *walked down the airport concourse* to my waiting plane. I was going home, but not to Garland, Texas, my dear hometown which held so many fond memories of growing up—of becoming. For only recently had I learned that I had another home—a place that I hailed from long before I had any conscious memory. I was going home to Colorado—the place where life began for me.

Tightly clutched in my arms—and unfortunately nudging an occasional passenger as I inched my way down the narrow airplane cabin aisle—was a long, white box containing a dozen red roses. They matched a single red rose pinned to the lapel of my brown suit—an outfit painstakingly chosen for this day that would change my life forever. The roses were a symbolic response to a childhood friend's comments made each Mother's Day—an annual, gut-wrenching dilemma that no one but an adopted person like me could understand. "Now remember, when they pass out roses to wear on your dress at church on Mother's Day, you'll have to wear a white rose since your first mother is dead," she would chant.

Today I wore and bore my red roses proudly—an answer at last to her well-meaning yet haunting suggestion.

Only a few days before I boarded the plane—for the first time in my life—I had looked at the face of an adult whom I physically resembled. The photos of my birth mother, who was not dead as my childhood friend had presumed but was in the prime of an active life as a schoolteacher in Colorado, arrived in the mail. They were greeted by shrieks of joy and wonder by my husband Louis and young son Matthew, who peered at the face that stared at him from the photograph and mused, "So that's where I get my big brown eyes!"

They also were greeted with rejoicing by my adoptive parents, who to my immense relief were my biggest cheerleaders when only six weeks before I fearfully made the announcement. I had decided to begin a search for my birth family since neither my parents nor I knew one detail about my birth heritage.

> *Many of the missing threads in the tapestry of my life seemed to reappear in an instant.*

No words could describe the drama of that initial phone call when, after several weeks of inquiring and help from an intermediary, I heard for the first time the voice of Eleanor, the woman who had given life to but who never had held nor even seen the child for whom she made an adoption plan in 1948.

In that awkward yet fulfilling phone conversation, where the words to years of pent-up questions couldn't pour out fast enough, many of the missing threads in the tapestry of my life seemed to reappear in an instant. I was awed by some of the physical similarities she described. I thrilled to know that I—reared as an only child—had a sister. And when I learned that I hailed from a family of journalists, I was overwhelmed by the coincidence, since I worked as *Houston Chronicle* reporter and had written voraciously from early childhood.

But as we talked, it became obvious that one phone call was not enough to fill a lifetime of gaps. We promised to exchange photos, and in her photo package that arrived by mail was an invitation: Hop on a plane and come to Colorado next weekend. So now I was on my way—excited, ecstatic, fearful, numb—experiencing the full range of human emotions as my plane drew closer to its destination.

> *I could not fathom the searing questions that the next few days would raise...*

Searing Questions to Come

Flying on the airplane on that historic day, I could not fathom the searing questions that the next few days' events would raise nor the fact that these questions would take years and even decades to process. They were questions such as—

❧ What goes on in a birth mother's mind when she makes an adoption plan for a child she carries? What does she think on the child's birthday? How does she grieve this loss?

❧ Are adopted individuals curious about birth fathers, and would I eventually want to find mine? And do birth fathers ever wonder what happened to their children, too?

❧ How would I explain this story to Matthew, who was now three and too young to fully grasp its import, and to other children we might have as the years went by?

❧ Would my godly, Christian parents, although supportive now, continue to be pleased about my decision after the initial drama died down? Would they, in the end, think me ungrateful for the loving home God provided for me? And how would that affect our long-term relationship, which all my life had been nothing but affirming and loving?

❧ Would this visit be just the beginning of a long and enduring association between me and my birth family, or would one or all of us choose to sever the relationship after this initial meeting?

❧ How would these new family members feel about the bulldozing of a stranger into their lives? And how would they explain my existence to others?

❧ How would I process this new infusion of information about myself, as I added whole new layer of facts about the "me" that I was discovering to the "me" that I had known for the past 30 years?

❧ Would my husband and friends support me if this reunion experience had some unforeseen impact on me emotionally, or would they resent me for having rocked the boat and grow weary and irritated with me in the process?

❧ Would these events have any impact on my Christian testimony, and would my Christian faith play any part in my reaction to these new turns in my life?

❧ Was this process of finding my birth family really healthy, or would everyone be better off without this information?

❧ And finally, what could be done to prevent the anxiety created when mothers give birth to children whom they cannot rear? And what can be done to help adoptive parents who, like mine, want to share information but don't know any, or who fear the outcome too much to give their consent or to tell what they know?

A Nationwide Movement

As it turned out, I was one of the first among many people who would be asking questions like these during the next two decades. Although no exact figure exists on the number of adoptees who today have found or are seeking their birth roots, the baby boom era spawned more than 6 million adoptions in the 30-year period since World War II. [1] This created an enormous pool of people with the potential to either do or be affected by exactly what I was doing on my historic airplane journey. What I was experiencing was one person's pilgrimage in a nationwide movement that was beginning to consume all parties in the adoption triad—adopted persons, adoptive parents, and birth family.

Like a great tidal wave, social changes have swept over the whole adoption process in the United States.

Nationwide groups such as Adoptees Liberty Movement Association, formed in the late 1970s to help adopted persons like me who desired to know more about their birth families. They claimed that it is unreal for adopted persons to continue to deny the existence of those who literally gave them lives. Eventually these groups would begin to consider their cause to shatter this wall of secrecy to be a civil rights movement. And Concerned United Birthparents, another national group, formed about the same time to help birth mothers like mine who were found, as well as those who wanted to learn more about the children they bore and no longer wanted to be separated from.

Like a great tidal wave, social changes of monumental proportion have swept over the whole adoption process throughout the United States, creating new forms of relationships and new approaches to adoption not often seen before the late 1970s.

Adoption once was an all-or-nothing proposition. All contact between birth family and adoptive parents was irrevocably severed; the adopted child was supposed to pretend that his adoptive parents were his only parents, and birth mothers were supposed to agree never to lay eyes on their child in the future. But the scene is slowly changing. Open adoption, in which birth and adoptive parents may meet and maintain whatever relationship is comfortable for them, is growing increasingly popular. Support groups, businesses, and non-profit organizations that help adoptees and birth parents contact each other have become an emerging industry in this country. Even agencies still lukewarm to open adoption now maintain registries in which birth parents or adopted persons who want to be found may keep their names on file in case the other party in their case desires a match-up.

Some states now have varying degrees of open adoption records that give adult adoptees access to their sealed birth records or at least limited rights to petition a court for certain information. And in reaction to some well-publicized cases where adoptions have been ended by court order after birth parents changed their minds and fought for return of their babies, many are pushing for adoption reform that would make all states' adoption laws more specific and more uniform.

The Pro-Life Movement's fight against abortion and the Supreme Court's 1973 Roe v. Wade decision have sparked a positive re-emphasis on the need to provide homes for the potential adopted persons who are spared execution in the womb. Although some pro-choice groups have decried adoption out of fear they would lend credibility to right-to-life forces, others are starting to look more positively at adoption as another key option for sparing infertile women's bodies from years of sometimes denigrating fertility technology. And because the culture that once sent unwed expectant mothers scurrying for anonymity in sequestered places has given way to a more tolerant and open society toward single mothers, new forms of adoption plans are needed.

Questions Remain the Same

Despite all that has transpired, parties in the adoption triad still have many of the same questions they did at the onset of all these changes. Today, however, these cultural shifts have caused far more people to ask the questions and to feel more free about posing them.

After my experiences with finding my birth family prompted the *Houston Chronicle* to print my three-part, first-person adoption series, (which was nominated for a Pulitzer Prize), my office telephone rang for a solid month with questions from people affected by all aspects of adoption. Requests poured in for me to speak locally and nationally (including one from a San Antonio adoption agency that felt the issues were so urgent that I was asked to talk only ten days after the birth of our second child, Catharine). Then, as now, the scope of questions remains the same.

They come from—

❦ Adopted persons of all ages—who want to know whether their bottled-up feelings of curiosity are normal; whether, when, and how when they should search; how a reunion would affect them; how to deal lovingly with their adoptive parents; what will happen after a reunion occurs; how they deal with the information they find, and how they relate to the new branches of the family tree that they locate in the process.

❦ Birth parents—who wonder whether they should initiate a search, how they should respond if they're found, whether that child they relinquished will despise them for a decision made long ago, how they can explain to their families the sudden appearance on the scene of a birth daughter or son, what kind and degree of contact would be healthy, whether they as expectant parents should choose an agency that has an open adoption, or whether they should choose adoption at all.

❦ And adoptive parents—even those who adopted in more recent years and were provided much non-identifying information on their child—are wondering what information they should share with their children, how and when they should share it, whether to support an adoptee-birth family reunion, and whether it will affect the long-term relationship they will have with their adopted son or daughter.

Tips from Others

To provide a resource like this book that would answer those questions, I decided to seek out other parties in the adoption process and find out how they've dealt with various issues in their lives. I interviewed adoptive parents whose children are newborn, as well as adoptive parents of grown children about what techniques worked best for them. I talked to contemporary adoptive parents who know little more birth family information than mine did in the late 1940s as well as adoptive parents whose recent adoptions are so open that they receive regular letters or visits from their children's birth mothers.

Adopted individuals I interviewed range from one who, although still in elementary school, is highly articulate in describing physical traits of her birth family, to an adult adopted person who thinks the whole concept of gleaning biological information is unnecessary. Birth parents with whom I spoke ranged from one who initiated the reunion with her daughter to one who struggled with the ramifications of being found—and yet came to acceptance.

I talked to parents who adopted children from abuse situations and who discussed how they will deal with their children's queries about birth family. I interviewed one couple who adopted from a foreign country and have visited that country to see how much family heritage information they can acquire. I talked to adoption social workers who work regularly with all parties in the adoption triad and members of search groups who try to help parties seeking information.

Those I interviewed shared with me in nuts-and-bolts terms how they have dealt with adoption-related issues in their lives. They gave specific examples of how they've answered their children's questions and at what age they think certain approaches are appropriate. They gave special insights of how they felt or currently feel about growing up adopted and how they feel people helped or are helping them through the process.

They talked about the joys and challenges of connecting with their birth families and how people in their lives such as spouses, friends, and church leaders, supported them. Most of all, they shared how their faith in God has sustained them through infertility and long waits for placement, seemingly fruitless searches, unplanned pregnancies, separation from children after birth, tedious *From my personal experience and what I have learned from others, the cost is worth the effort to learn the answers that provide a complete and fulfilling life.* post-reunion adjustments, child rearing challenges, and other special issues that only those related to adoption know.

Out of their experiences, and out of my own rich adoption history, including my veteran's perspective on finding and knowing my birth family, I'll share some answers and tips that have worked for people who have wrestled with the same questions. I will also share a special list of groups, agencies, books, and other resources that exist to help people with adoption-related issues today. And at the end of each chapter, which includes my story plus those of others, I'll provide a summary of tips that pertain to the issues discussed in that chapter.

The tips (listed by categories beginning with chap. 2) will show how each of the three parties in the adoptive triad—adopted persons, adoptive parents, birth parents—can respond to the aspect of adoption that chapter explores.

For me, and for the people I interviewed, finding workable answers to adoption-related questions is not easy and not always without heartache. But from my personal experience and what I have learned from others, the cost is worth the effort to learn the answers that provide a complete and fulfilling life. I'm thankful that I was in the vanguard of this movement so that I can share this perspective with others still on the journey.

Unfurling a New Era

But the fact that I was on the cutting edge of a nationwide movement or was about to take part in an event that would have reverberations for me for years to come was the furthest matter from my mind that day as my plane drew closer to its landing at the Colorado airport.

I had traveled to this state as a child. I had taken the usual Rocky Mountain sightseeing tour with my parents and never suspected that I had been here before, after a fashion.

> *Those craggy, snow-rimmed peaks of my first home state reached out with beckoning arms as my plane descended.*

But now, with the truth of my origins in my hand, those craggy, snow-rimmed peaks of my first home state reached out with beckoning arms as my plane descended.

I had seen a T. S. Elliott poem that said, "And at the end of all our exploring will be to arrive where we started. . . And know the place for the first time."[2] Arriving in Colorado was, in every sense, a homecoming yet seen for the first time through the new eyes of the "me" I was discovering.

I waited until the entire plane emptied of passengers before I began gathering my belongings. My first consideration for waiting was practical—I wanted to avoid bonking any more passengers as I reached into the overhead luggage compartment to retrieve my box of roses and inched my way down the plane aisle as I carried my unwieldy, oversized package. My husband often teased me that I never did anything in a normal way—everything had to have some element of the dramatic, and this meticulously planned reunion with my birth mother was certainly not going to be an exception to my lifelong Sarah Bernhard-esque penchant.

A whole new era in my life was potentially about to unfurl on the other side of the airline's exit door.

But the second reason for dallying related to a last-minute case of the jitters, plain and simple. What if I emerged from the plane, walked into a crowd of waiting people, and saw no one that even remotely resembled the woman in the photograph? I reasoned that if I were the last to exit to plane, the crowd surely would have thinned by then. By process of elimination, fewer people would be in the waiting area to see if anyone answered to the name of Eleanor if no face immediately matched the one I sought.

Then came the a second, even sicker feeling. What if my birth mother and her family suddenly got a last-minute case of the jitters themselves—so jittery, in fact, that they decided to forego the whole reunion? In my wallet were pertinent phone numbers, including those of other contacts in the Colorado city that friends had rounded up for me just in case I needed another place to stay. But if this worst-case scenario occurred—and if I were at the tail-end of the disembarking passengers—I concluded that fewer people would be around to witness my embarrassment and tears of disappointment.

With all these eventualities sloshing around in my head, I gathered up my tote bag and my roses and exited the by-then-empty plane. A whole new era in my life was potentially about to unfurl on the other side of the airline's exit door.

Using This Chapter

Adoption affects all the parties involved in adoption across their lifespans. An event that may seem a one-time occurrence for the adopted parents, adopted child, and birth parents actually will have ripple effects throughout the lives of each member of the "adoption triad," as this collection of parties to adoption has come to be called. Adopted individuals, birth parents, and adoptive parents are all connected and will be throughout their lives—whether or not any members of the constellation ever choose to meet. Without the birth parents no child would exist. Without the child, no adoptive parents would be on the scene. Whether anyone likes it or not, children are born into an original family. They will at some point in their lives face that fact even if in facing it they determine that they do nothing about it in terms of knowing the flesh-and-blood people involved.

Adopted individuals, birth parents, and adoptive parents are all connected and will be throughout their lives—whether or not any members of the constellation ever choose to meet.

Members of an adoptive family that claim nothing different exists about their family by virtue of the fact that an adopted person is a member of it kid themselves—in the same way stepfamilies invite disaster if their members do not acknowledge that some highly different dynamics were at play in the way their family was formed. These unique challenges are not hurdles to be run from but are growing edges that can be acknowledged and met head-on with integrity.

The Questions:
Growing Up Adopted

🌿

*M*y *childhood friend's reminder that* prompted the red roses I carried was one of seemingly hundreds of "teasers" about my birth family that fell across my path during my growing-up years. Like many other adopted persons report, almost daily something popped up to alert me that I was genetically connected to another family apart from the one that reared me. And even as early as kindergarten days, those reminders absolutely consumed me with inquisitiveness.

When I was a preschooler, the arrival of the monstrous Dallas telephone directory probably held far more fascination for me than it did the average youngster. I recall tracing my fingers down column after column as I turned each tissue-thin page and wondering which of all those millions of surnames might have been mine originally.

Family gatherings also left an indelible mark on me. My adoptive mother was the youngest of three red-haired sisters—"the three little red-haired Miller girls"—as neighbors in their rural northeast Texas community dubbed them even into their senior years. Their carrot tops remained auburn into older adulthood and were a special badge to them—a link that said, "We belong to each other" and to their German-descent father, from whom they inherited them. With dark brown hair and hazel eyes, I felt I looked like an alien plunked down in their midst whenever we amassed for a family photograph.

But the annual trip to the dentist's office always dropped the biggest crumb, because it, unlike the other reminders, was tantamount to a live clue. Starting when I was about eight years old and began having dental X-rays taken, the ritual became predictable: The dentist examined my pictures, excitedly summoned his staff, and told them, "Look, she has some permanent teeth missing! Wow, Mother Nature played a dirty trick on her! Would you look at that!" He fingered a curious spot in my upper row of teeth and an identical spot in my lower row where a permanent tooth failed to form beneath each of my second bicuspids, right-hand side. The baby tooth in each spot would have nothing grow in to replace it when it fell out. "This runs in a family," he never failed to educate his onlookers each year as he made notes on my chart about this rarity.

A Thread in the Tapestry

For someone reared in the family into which he or she was born, that dentist's comment would mean nothing. It could be forgotten almost as quickly as could the unmemorable polish that dental hygienists used in those days, before today's flavorful choices like wild raspberry and chocolate mint.

But to an adoptee—especially one as insatiably curious as I was—the dentist might as well have handed me a piece of gold when he made that incidental comment about family traits. For what he had just done was to give me a genuine piece to the puzzle—one of the missing threads in the tapestry of my life.

I wanted to take that puzzle piece, leap from the dentist's chair, run out into the streets, and start prying open the mouths of everyone I met, saying, "Are you missing some permanent teeth? Are you missing some teeth?" Because even as an eight-year-old somehow I sensed that the information the dentist had just handed me might be just the link I needed someday to track down the people with whom I was biologically connected.

I began actually looking forward to my annual checkups just so I could hear the dentist replay that innocent, yet intoxicating, remark.

> *Mine was the most idyllic childhood anyone can imagine in the home of two people who were cookie-cutter models of loving, affirming parents.*

An Idyllic Childhood

Was this the tale of a child who had a bad adoption, who felt aloof or disconnected from her parents? Was this preoccupation with birth family at the root of some serious identity problems or maladjustment? Did it signify some immense lack of love on the part of those who were rearing me? It is easy to presume that if a child is curious, something is wrong with the adoptive family and that something is missing. But in thinking back over my life, those suggestions are almost laughable.

Mine was the most idyllic childhood anyone can imagine in the home of two people who were the cookie-cutter models of loving, affirming parents. Salt-of-the-earth, generous, and honest to a fault—my parents married during World War II, left their rural northeast Texas roots, and located in the growing Dallas suburb community of Garland, where my father was assistant postmaster and my mother was secretary to the city school superintendent.

Not only did many people in this town of two thousand know Mable and J. D. Wheeler because of their public roles, many people knew one other fact about them, too. They knew that this well-liked, good-natured couple who would make a model mom and dad could not have children born to them. As an older teen-ager—some twelve years before she would marry my dad—my mother had undergone a hysterectomy for a uterine tumor. My parents entered their marriage with the full knowledge that they well might be a childless duo. And by the time the war ended and life settled down for them enough to think about possibly adopting, their ages—thirty-seven and forty-four—put them past the qualifying limit for many agencies. My dad's dad, by then seventy, began to fear that his fondest dream of having a grandchild never would come true.

Then one morning in her Sunday School class, an acquaintance who knew their situation suggested that my mother contact a physician in town. "He's looking for a family to adopt a baby," the friend mentioned. Couple and doctor spoke, arrangements were made, and on November 13, 1948—my grandad's seventieth birthday—my mother called to tell him about his birthday gift, a three-day-old baby girl named Karen Kay. As was typical of adoptions in those days, the doctor handed me off to my parents without providing a shred of background information on my birth family. "Just take her home and love her, and she'll never want to know," was the prevailing viewpoint in adoptions of that era. And my parents, so delighted with their long-aited offspring, never dreamed that it would be important to ask.

> *As was typical of adoptions then, the doctor handed me to my parents without providing any background information on my birth family.*

Much Emotional Health

As an only child, an only grandchild on one side of the family, and one of only two grandchildren on the other, I never lacked attention. Although my parents were solid physical providers, the riches of my upbringing went beyond physical comforts. I was fortunate to be reared around much emotional health— around parents and other relatives who expressed appreciation openly, who permitted feelings to be expressed, and who brought me up to believe that I could do any-thing—literally anything I set my mind to do. My "Bandad" was so delighted over the grandchild he believed he would never have that he and my grandmother semi-monthly drove ninety miles to visit me. His pockets were always loaded with pennies for me to plunk into the gumball machine and his wallet supplied with bills to buy me whatever caught my eye at the dimestore.

> *I was fortunate to be reared around much emotional health—around people who expressed appreciation openly. . .*

But the rich environment that nurtured me extended be-yond the walls of our home, which my father carefully located within walking distance of schools and churches to accom-modate his family. It seemed that the entire community of Garland and the Baptist church in which I was reared literally enveloped me in a warm cocoon of love from the first day I arrived home as a tiny pink bundle in my mother's arms.

Cards and gifts poured in from well-wishers as word got out around town about the Wheelers' new baby. Almost from birth until my marriage twenty years later, the Garland daily newspaper ran a news item "every time you sneezed," as my husband put it years later as he pored over my mother's scrapbooks featuring stories of my accomplishments. From the time I was three and sang my first solo in front of the congregation, my precious church affirmed me, sought out my gifts, and launched me into adulthood with a solid biblical foundation and a rock-solid sense of self-worth that for years has held me in good stead.

Questions Abound

If ever a child existed that ostensibly should have no room to be curious about missing biological links, it was Kay Wheeler. And yet from my earliest memory, I would have given literally anything I owned to have known about my birth family.

Other adopted persons from warm, loving homes tell the same kinds of stories.

"My parents gave me the very best that life had to offer," said Kristen Cunningham, a social worker. "My birth mother had requested that I be placed in a home where I would have a solid religious upbringing and a good education. My parents certainly fulfilled all that. They sent me to a private Christian school. We're very close. Yet I had so many questions. I wondered why I had such a laid-back personality when everyone else in my family was a Type A. I felt like I had a creative streak that I couldn't seem to trace anywhere. It was a fundamental thing for me—needing to know who I am and where did I come from."

Court reporter Tana Hill tells the same type of story—a much loved daughter but one who always wondered where she got her height and musical abilities, since neither of those traits existed in her adoptive family.

"I was reared like a princess—this tremendously desired child," said Linda Sledge, coordinator of the children's program at a church. "I never lacked for a thing."

Three other adoptees who have found their birth families echoed these sentiments about their deep, abiding attachment to their adoptive families and how thoroughly loved they felt in their adoptive homes.

"I don't know how my parents could have loved me any more if I had been born to them," said hospital marketing director Jacqueline Jagger. "I always believed I was their special gift."

As time went on and inevitable questions came, my parents told me what they knew, which was absolutely nothing.

"I had a wonderful upbringing," said Mary A., a college professor, who asked that her last name not be used. "I never felt that I was a second-class child. I felt great that I was the first best thing that happened to them."

"I could never say anything negative about them," said Betsy DeShano, an administrative assistant. "I find myself repeating cliches that my dad instilled in me forever. I felt I was loved unconditionally."

Nor was the fact that I was adopted a matter that was hidden from me, as if it could be in a place like Garland where everyone knew my history anyway. The word "adopted" seemingly entered my vocabulary about the same time I was learning "dog" and "cat." And questions about adoption were handled matter-of-factly. My parents explained that I had first parents who could not keep me, that "Mommy and Daddy needed a baby and a doctor who knew that arranged for you to be in our home." As time went on and inevitable questions came, my parents told me what they knew, which was absolutely nothing.

Mary A. said, "I knew that my aunt got babies in her tummy and my mom got babies from the doctor. That was the way my adoption was explained to me, and it was a cute way of viewing it when you're a child. But I was still curious. I wanted to know *where* those babies that came from the doctor came from."

Convincing Replies

Although some adoptees describe a feeling of being thrown away by their original family, that was not an issue for me. When I posed questions about reasons why my first parents could not keep me, my mother replied convincingly, "I'm sure it was for a very good reason." As I matured, my mother elaborated possibilities on a level I could understand them. "She may not have had a husband. She may not have had a job. She may not have had a home," she would venture.

Paula Arrington tells of similar conversations with her adopted daughter Jenna, now a college student. "We always told her that her mother was very young, loved her very much, and made a wise plan for her, because she wanted her to have a mom and dad. That always seemed to satisfy her."

In their explanations, with their lack of specific facts, I never had a feeling that my parents were holding something from me. To them we were a family, and that was enough. Adoptee Susie Edwards, an administrative assistant in a denominational agency, echoed this exact sentiment when she discussed the reasons why she does not desire to search for her birth family.

"It just simply didn't matter to any of us," said Susie, one of three children adopted into her family. "My life was just too good. If things had turned out differently for me, I might have felt different. I had no need to be curious at all. My roots couldn't go any deeper. I don't have any ill feeling toward my birth parents. There had to be some reasons why they made this [adoption] plan for me, and if they were good enough for them then, they are good enough for me now. My adoptive mother never told me anything, and I never asked her. I didn't want them to think that their role in my life wasn't all that important." In her mind, life began when her adoptive parents entered the scene, and that was all she needed. She said family traits held absolutely no fascination for her—not as a child nor as an adult.

Just the opposite was true for me, however. During my grade-school years, my imagination worked overtime. Sometimes I would envision my birth mother as a movie star; at other times I thought of her as a princess. Like many adoptees, I wondered if the arrival of my birthdate each year brought my birth mother memories. But always, she was there in my fantasy, and inquiring grade-school friends who knew of my adoption were always around to fan the flames.

Treasured Adoption Lore

To accompany their always candid, always age-appropriate explanations about being adopted, my parents did an especially sound job of providing me a legacy of what I call my "adoption lore"—stories that my own children can repeat almost verbatim even today—that from an early age helped incorporate my adoption into my identity.

Especially precious to me is the story of my dad's early attempt to hold me while my mother freed her hands to warm a bottle on the day they brought me home from the hospital as an infant. Clearly decades before equal-opportunity parenting, he squirmed a little when my mother asked for his help and replied incredulously, "You mean you want me to hold that little thing?" My mother's descriptions of his awkward yet tender attempts that followed are words indelibly pressed on my mind.

Likewise the immortal story of my mother's 1948 surprise call to "Bandad," informing him that, "We haven't had time to get a birthday gift for you, Mr. Wheeler, but we have a special present we think you'll like even more than you would a shirt and tie," was recited to me from an early age and made me feel special and wanted and cherished and rare.

But no matter how treasured the stories and no matter how enchanting the lore, lurking behind them always was the question in my mind, "But who? But when? But why?" They were questions about who and what came first—before the call to "Bandad," before my mother's first formula bottle. And no one and nothing—not even all the love in the world—could fill the gaps, those missing pieces of identity that I felt must be filled.

Teen-Age Concerns

During my teen years, as homogeneity with peers became crucial, I mentally put my adopted status on the back burner. It wasn't that I had any less of an interest in my roots; my passion simply went underground. No longer did it feel "special" for my friends to mention my adoption in public. It would put me in the category of "different," which most adolescents dread.

Often during this life stage, many adolescent adoptees treat their parents to a guilt-inducing harangue of statements like, "If I lived with my real mother, she wouldn't make me do those chores," or "You don't have any right to take that privilege away from me. I'm really not your child." For some teen-agers those are not just idle words; some feel estranged enough to leave home over issues that they feel stem from their adoption.

Pastor's wife Cookie Hays said that although their adopted daughter, Margaret Mary, is several years away from being a teen-ager, this eight-year-old "knows how to push my buttons" when she's angry and upset and sometimes will remind Cookie, "You're not my real mother."

"I try to have the same reaction that any parent would when their child says hurtful things," says Cookie. "I just try to stay calm, not react visibly, and tell her over and over, 'I love you, and I always will.'"

Lashing out at my parents with a heart-rending charge like this was not one of my teen-age ruses. As an adolescent I simply and suddenly stopped wanting anyone to know about my adoption origins. When I was twelve or thirteen and my mother won a community service award, I shocked her by asking her not to mention during her newspaper interview the fact that I was adopted. That bit of information just was not something that a teen-ager wanted to have broadcast. I am sure my sudden lack of interest in being adopted was puzzling from a child who once stood on a downtown Dallas department store counter and chirped to the world, "I'm Mommy's cookie and Daddy's angel and Mommy and Daddy's adopted baby." But it was a scenario that is not uncommon for teen-aged adopted persons.

When friends boasted about eating their mom's Italian cooking or about owning their family's Scottish plaid, I felt strangely cheated.

Once in college, however, I found that my being adopted made me seem somewhat novel and interesting among new acquaintances. Roommates queried me for hours about my unknown past.

In Search of Ethnicity

Ignorance about national origin particularly irked me, since by the time I reached young adulthood I determined that I was very ethnic looking. When friends boasted about eating their mom's Italian cooking or about owning their family's Scottish plaid, I felt strangely cheated. It didn't seem fair for some people to be able to write college research papers tracing their family trees back seven generations to some historical figure, while I could not even trace my biological roots back one.

On a summer tour of Europe and the Middle East, my college chums agreed to survey facial features in each country we visited to see which group I most resembled. Feeling sorry for me because I did not know my nationality, they decided to give me one. At the end of the tour and after culling out features from each group, Italian was their choice, followed by French and Lebanese.

> *Basking in the praise of my family, I always felt that just one more person, my original mother, should know about these rites of passage in my life.*

Back home a short while later, I filled my car up at an Italian-owned service station. A dark youth peered at me through the glass as he cleaned the window, then stuck his head into the car, and asked, "You Italian, too?"

"Sure," I replied, remembering the poll results but feeling a little untruthful.

I continued to collect genetic traits in a way that non-adoptees never could understand. Always in the back of my mind was the dentist's pronouncement about my congenital baby teeth. And the dermatologist who told me he was removing the "always familial" white moles from my face could not understand why I smiled all the way through the Novocaine shots.

The birth mother figure loomed heavy again during any milestone in my life—marriage, graduation, job success. Basking in the praise of my family, I always felt that just one more person, my original mother, should know about these rites of passage in my life. Paula Arrington said daughter Jenna shared similar views at one point when she began to think about marriage. "There's something about this kind of life event that seems to prompt it," Paula said.

Missing Health Factors

When Louis and I lost our first child through stillbirth, my need to reach out for my origins hit its first peak. In my desolation, I sentimentally likened myself to a dandelion, whose wispy white fuzz was here today, gone tomorrow. Not only did I know no bone-of-my-bone person who came before me, but I also might never leave a physical antecedent whom I could look at and say, "This person truly is a part of me." I felt I was genetically connected to no one on earth and possibly never would be.

And physicians during that sad period in my life only seemed to add insult to injury. In trying to determine genetic factors that would help them advise me about a subsequent pregnancy, a doctor glared across the table at me and said, "Don't you know any family medical history at all?" as though I were some kind of sideshow freak instead of an adoptee simply shut off from that part of her past. Other adoptees report watching doctors ceremoniously rip up medical history sheets in front of them and making them feel like second-class citizens for reporting honestly, "I can't give you any information. I'm adopted."

Not that agencies and physicians who helped birth mothers make adoption plans in the 1940s and 1950s maliciously withheld family medical history from adoptive parents. In those days family medical history simply was not deemed as important in health screening, early diagnosis, treatment, and reproductive decision-making. Today much more is known about the role that genetics play in these matters. So the agencies and physicians who espoused, "Just take her home and love her and she'll never need to know"—even medical information—came by that prevailing viewpoint honestly, based on everything that was known about heredity and environment in those days. They could not have envisioned the great groundswell that would occur years later when those children, all grown up, would feel desperately cut off from vital information and would be determined to marshal it.

From the time I was eleven I felt called by God to be a Christian journalist—long before I knew of any birth family link to that profession. I had claimed as one of my life verses John 18:37, "For this I have been born, and for this I have come into the world, to bear witness to the truth. Every one who is of the truth hears My voice" NASB. This verse was Christ's testimony before Pilate, but I felt it pretty well summed up my purpose in terms of my writing career. But now that I was among the adult adoptees in that groundswell, it was only natural that that verse would begin to apply to my need for truth of my origins. For someone whose life was devoted to such a cause, what else but the truth of my past would satisfy?

So on that long-awaited day I carried a bouquet of roses down the jetway that in a few short minutes could link me with those life-long questions. But a dandelion bouquet would have been just as apt a symbol for those long, frustrating days in the dark. Growing up adopted, even in the most loving and caring of circumstances, was a struggle for connectedness—not just a wispy, ephemeral kind of existence—that for me could be eased only by knowing flesh and blood.

Using This Chapter

Adopted Persons

❦ Do not feel guilty if you are not curious, but do not bury your feelings either. Curiosity is normal, but not all adoptees are curious, nor should they be.

❦ Be prepared when life events, such as graduation, marriage, or other significant developments occur. These can trigger an onset of pent-up questions. If these questions surface, be prepared to ask them.

Adoptive Parents

❦ Explain adoption as early and as straightforwardly as possible. Doing so adds to your credibility and prevents the possibility of someone else telling your child first; it also makes adoption seem a fact of life. Helping children understand the truth of their heritage helps them understand to be truthful in life.

❧ Be completely prepared for the day when your child asks for more information about his or her birth family. Provide information as it is asked in the same way you would about sex, religion, or other personal matters. Information about nationality and physical traits of birthparents seem especially important to children. Reassure your children that no reason exists for them to feel hesitant or ashamed to inquire. But do not overemphasize it either.

❧ Avoid negative comments about the birth family. Children need to know that they were born of essentially good people and that they were not rejected because of who they are.

❧ Do not presume that children are not interested because they do not ask. Have books around the house on adoption, and look for teachable moments.

❧ Do not think you are going to do such a great job rearing children that they will not want to know about their birth family or even search. Whether they do or do not has nothing to do with what kind of parenting job you did. You cannot inoculate someone against curiosity. Remember that standing in the way of a child's obtaining such information is a sure-fire ticket to helping parent and child drift apart.

❧ When children shout hurtful things, do not presume it is because you have failed as a parent. Look for the real message behind the statement. Try to talk about why children are hurting. Sometimes they may be asking whether you care enough about them and whether your ties to them are strong enough to make them obey. Children from both adoptive and birth families have arguments with parents; all children figure out the best ways they know to irritate parents at times.

❀ Expect a decline in adoption interest during the teen-age years. Teens do not want to be thought of as different. A lack of interest has nothing to do with their attitude or even curiosity about adoption but merely reflects on their stage in life.

Birth Parents

❀ Realize that adoptive parents by and large treat the subject of the birth family with tender care. Many birth parents fear they've been vilified in the eyes of their children, but this is rarely the case. A brief chat with a child who is adopted is testimonial to this: Children use respectful terms to speak of birth parents, which is a sincere reflection of how their parents have dealt with this subject. The most common answer—and probably the best—that adoptive parents give to children's inquiries is "I don't know" if they truly don't.

❀ Decide whether you are willing to be found or whether you will initiate a search when and if the right time comes. In either situation don't try to go it alone. Seek help from your agency or from books on the subject like this one or others referenced in this book's appendix that will truly give you all the pros and cons and hows and wherefores of each situation. Already be thinking about what degree of contact you would tolerate and what closed doors still stand in your way.

T H R E E

The Families:
The Ties That Bind

❧

*T*he pilgrimage that led to the walk down the airplane jetway actually began to build its first serious momentum during the period after our childbirth loss. Before that time, I never had given much thought to how I would put feet to my interest in tracing my origins. But in that naturally introspective era when Louis and I were back to square one in terms of building the family of our future, I began to take the first mental steps toward tracking down the family of my past.

As I strategized, I reasoned that finding my birth family actually might be a simple process for me for two reasons. To begin with, I had reported on civil courts for several years for the *Houston Chronicle* and had an insider's knowledge on some aspects of the process. Although many states, including Texas at that time, still sealed adoption records, I knew that certain court files during my particular era still had both birth mother's and adoptive parents' names listed in the adoption petition. And secondly, the physician who helped my birth mother with her adoption plan in 1948 still was practicing in my hometown. I reasoned that if I could muster my courage to visit him, he might remember and share some details.

But at this point, the faces of my adoptive family—so cherished, so dear—always entered the picture. I was sure the doctor would alert my parents instantly if I appeared at his office asking questions. However great was my anguish over the need to know, the anguish of hurting my parents was greatest of all.

"Whose insides did I kick? Whose waistline did I expand? Whom did I cause to cry out in labor?"

The courthouse route would have to do, I thought, as I made plane reservations to fly from Houston and spend the day in Dallas, where my records would be. I would visit the courthouse without calling my parents. I would search the records and return home.

But as time drew near for my trip, so did bouts of morning sickness. I was pregnant again and, fearing that the stress of what I was about to undertake might cause a second childbirth loss, I jettisoned the idea of the trip.

Plagued with Questions

With this pregnancy, my inquisitiveness hit another high ebb—the same story Linda Sledge tells about what prompted her to search for her birth family. As this unborn child, highly active (unlike the first one), kicked and stirred, I was plagued with questions, "Whose insides did *I* kick? Whose waistline did *I* expand? Whom did *I* cause to cry out in labor?"

Linda says she wondered about genetic defects. She said her husband Tim's brother has cystic fibrosis and she wondered if she also might be a carrier. "We knew about things on his side of the family, but we knew nothing about mine," she said. She began her search just before she became pregnant with her first child.

In my case, fear for the safety of my pregnancy halted all thoughts of continuing a search, or so I thought. After my son arrived safe and healthy, at last I could look at his tiny face and spot features that were mine. With this new offspring, I now was only half a dandelion, and I reasoned that I should be content with that status. Again, my fears of alienating my parents made me feel thoughtless, heartless, and ungrateful at even entertaining the idea. A verse from Psalms kept coming to mind: "The lines are fallen unto me in pleasant places; yea, I have a goodly heritage" (Ps. 16:6). I reasoned I should be content with the goodly heritage I knew I had and that I should let go of my other needs.

A Dramatic Assignment

As Houston began to feel ripples from the adoption rights movement in the late 1970s, my editor, who knew I had some personal knowledge of the subject, quite naturally assigned to me stories when adopted persons began in large numbers to reunite with their birth families. I always empathized with the need for open adoption records and the adoptee's need to know—and my empathy helped me to write sensitively and well.

I always was careful, however, never to disclose my own adopted status to anyone I interviewed. Somehow, I feared someone might press me to change my mind from a no-search decision I believed now was firm.

That was until I received the assignment to travel south of Houston to LaMarque, Texas, to visit Winnie Ferguson. California artist Marty Renault, a daughter for whom Winnie had made an adoption plan forty years before, had recently found Winnie. By that point I already had covered several such adoption reunion dramas. I told my editor that too many of these soap-operas could amount to overkill. I started to toss this latest reunion fact sheet into the waste basket.

But she had another point of view. "Kay, you know the readers will love it. Just look at the drama here," she prevailed. "It could be the best-read thing in the section Sunday. Hop to it." The next day I checked out a *Chronicle* car and headed south for the interview that for all times would change my opinion about adopted person/birth family reunions and their effects on adoptive parents.

Winnie Ferguson was a walking smile when she greeted me at her home in LaMarque. Back from her reunion with daughter Marty in California only a few weeks before, she was basking in euphoria.

As with all other reunion stories I covered, I found my eyes misting as Winnie played Marty's tape recording of the first phone conversation between the two women.

In the tape, Marty told Winnie, "I was born at Hepzibah Home in Louisiana on April 22, 1938, and I believe I am your daughter."

And as with other reunions, I read the heartwarming letters the two women exchanged in the days that followed, and I talked with Winnie's husband Bill, who also was overjoyed by the event.

I smiled when she pointed to a highly protruding bone on her wrist. "You see this bone? Everyone in my family has one; it's sort of our trademark. Same thing with those brown moles. Both of my daughters have them. Well, for years, I looked at every pretty girl I saw to see if she might also have the same funny bone and these moles."

And although I still said nothing to give myself away, I was reminded afresh of the years I also had scanned crowds to find someone with my "familial" white moles and the missing permanent teeth.

"Just Good People"

Then Winnie held out a picture. Marty was standing in the middle of two women—Winnie on the left and Marty's adoptive mother on the right. Marty had introduced them during Winnie's California trip.

"Her adoptive mother totally supported her in this search," said Winnie. "When the picture was taken, Marty said, 'I now have two wonderful mothers.'"

"Supported her?" I gasped. "I can't believe it." Was her adoptive mother trained in psychology, so that she had some vast, superior understanding of the adoption phenomenon? What kind of family could be so unthreatened, so generous?

Had the Lord enabled me to cross paths with Winnie that day to give me some answers to the struggle that burned inside me?

Winnie replied that she didn't think Marty's family had some special training that prepared them for this monumental event.

"They are just good people," she said.

Just good people, I thought. Didn't my family certainly fit into that category? Was it possible that all my fears about my parents were based totally on assumption? I'd never even talked to them about my need to know these matters that were at the core of my existence. Did I really have any sound reason to believe I would anger them, alienate them, or lose their love? Had the Lord enabled me to cross paths with Winnie that day to give me some answers to the struggle that burned inside me?

No Turning Back

My husband Louis, like me, was a reporter on the *Houston Chronicle.* He was aware of the assignment I had that morning. In fact, before I departed for any of these reunion assignments, he always queried me about whether I would come back set to do my own search.

Arriving back from the visit with Winnie in LaMarque, I slid briskly past Louis' desk and avoided his eyes as I arrived back at the *Chronicle*. But I didn't move fast enough.

"Hey, how did it go? Have a good time?" he queried.

Then he took one look at my red-rimmed eyes, which told him the whole story.

The die was cast. We both knew what I had to do. And there could be no turning back.

Fearing a Breach

Other adopted individuals report similar periods of concern about telling their adoptive parents about decisions to search. Kristen Cunningham's adoptive parents knew from Kristen's early childhood that her birth mother desired to keep up with Kristen's development anonymously through the agency. "My parents always told me that they figured I'd probably meet my birth mother someday," she said. Kristen said her parents always cooperated with the agency and sent her birth mother Wendy frequent, but nonidentifying, reports about Kristen's growing interests and development. She said they knew the agency passed on the information to Wendy, a nurse, and Wendy in turn communicated medical information about herself through the agency to them.

Yet when Kristen, as a college student, was offered the opportunity to begin corresponding with Wendy, she wondered how it would impact her adoptive parents.

"They'd been so open about it all along, but when it came time to actually make the contact, I said, 'Wow, this is a big leap.'" Kristen says she remembers praying in the library chapel at her university about whether it was God's will that she initiate this contact and about her parents' reaction. "I just felt confident in my relationship with them (her parents)," Kristen said. "I had a love for Wendy before I knew her, so it wasn't like anyone's love was displaced." She said knowing Wendy was "just another person to love in your life—not like a love I have for my parents. I hoped that they would see it as if I was contacting a long-lost friend."

Linda Sledge said her first priority in deciding to search for her birth family was to protect her adoptive parents. "I didn't want them to feel abandoned; for one thing, we don't have much [adoptive] family, and I was everything to them." She said she would have "dropped the search at any time" if her parents indicated they felt she was deserting them.

In writing about his experiences, Richard Weizel recalled that people at the Manhattan adoption agency where he searched "told me I shouldn't, that I had a good family and ought to be grateful. I was grateful, but that didn't change my need to know my birth mother. For a year I did virtually nothing but search, spending up to eighteen hours a day playing private investigator and even hiring one" in his efforts to find his birth family.[1]

Just the Right Ruse

It was several weeks before I could think of just the right ruse to talk to my adoptive parents about my need to search for my birth mother. Although I basically had good, open communication with my parents, this subject seemed too fragile to be broached without some careful entree. I prayed that God would give me the right words to communicate love for them as well as my need to know. But when a game plan came to mind, it always seemed too simple.

Then one day I received a brochure about the Adoptees Liberty Movement Association (ALMA), an organization of adult adoptees in this country. ALMA was planning a national conference in May in California. Lots of big guns in the adoptees' movement would be attending; it would be a perfect background for my newspaper stories about reunions and the like. The *Chronicle* agreed to send me.

But there was a secondary method to my madness. Such an important trip hardly could be kept from my parents, who lived in Garland but still kept general track of my comings and going. I now had the entree I needed to open Pandora's box. I thanked God for helping this plan fall into my lap and continued to pray for just the right moment to appear.

> *Surely, after such a tender time with loved ones, no one could doubt my devotion to this family that had nurtured me since childhood.*

The appointed time occurred on my next trip to Garland, just after Easter. My family and I had just returned home from a sentimental day in Cooper, the small town where my parents were reared and where many of my relatives still lived. We spent the day looking through old family pictures and walking down memory lane with my aunts, uncle, and cousins. Surely, after such a tender time with loved ones, no one could doubt my devotion to this family that had nurtured me since childhood.

When Mother and I were alone that evening, I gingerly told her about the *Chronicle* business trip.

"It's a group called ALMA. That stands for Adoptees Liberty Movement Association. Have you ever heard of them?"

I already knew the answer, since my parents are avid newspaper readers and television news watchers. The vast number of ALMA stories in the news media lately would not have escaped them.

The Gift of Life All Over

My mother's face at first became very stern. The lines around her mouth went hard, and she was silent. *Here comes the lecture,* I thought, gritting my teeth.

Then a strange thing happened. An almost mirthful smile came on her lips, she lifted her eyes, and her face erupted into a grin. Something about it told me that a huge weight had just been lifted from her shoulders.

"Oh, I'm so glad you asked. You know your daddy and I read all those adoption stories and have wondered why in the world you weren't interested in searching like those people have," she exclaimed.

If she had told me that she, at age 68, was pregnant, I would not have been more shocked.

"You mean you wouldn't be mad?"

"Mad?" It was as though the thought never crossed her mind. "Do you know what? Your daddy and I already had decided that we were going to talk with the doctor who placed you and get all the information, write it up, and put it with our wills, so you could find it after we were gone. I'd be curious about my past if I were you. Besides, Daddy and I wanted you to be left with some family after we departed this earth."

"But why didn't you tell me you felt this way?" I stammered, still in disbelief.

"Because you never asked. When you were in high school, you didn't want to talk about adoption. So we decided that we wouldn't bring up the subject unless you asked first. We didn't want to hurt your feelings."

I was struck with the total incredulity of it all. Suddenly I saw that the years of inaction and worry on both our parts were based solely on assumption. My parents' concept of my attitude about adoption never had emerged past my teen-age years, when I went through a denial period about my "different" status. And my assumptions about my parents were based on my own unasked questions. For a journalist, such poor communication was unpardonable.

But my period of self-flagellating was short-lived because of my euphoria. My mother and, a few short minutes later, my daddy, had given me the release I needed. They loved me enough to turn me loose. Whatever decisions I made next about the specifics of how to pursue the search I was determined to make, I could do with the knowledge that I had not just their blessing but also their encouragement. When they adopted me thirty years before, they had given me the gift of life—a life rich in provisions and affirmation and spiritual depth and love. By turning me loose to search for birth family, it was as though they had given me the gift of life all over again. The verse in Psalms that I had clung to was more applicable now than ever. I truly did "have a goodly heritage," as the Scripture said.

Other Reactions

Linda Sledge said her father, as he lay dying of pancreatic cancer, gave her the same kind of message about finding her birth family. Totally unprompted by Linda, and during a time when all attention was focused on his health and comfort, her father suddenly turned to her and volunteered, "You are the best thing that ever happened to us. If you find your [birth] mother, tell her 'thank you' for me."

Not all adopted persons find adoptive parents so open to their quests. In the early days of the adoption reform movement, and especially just after my three-part series in the *Houston Chronicle* held my parents up as role models of openness and tolerance on this subject—I received calls by the score from adoptive parents demanding to know, "How could you? And how could your parents let you do such a thing?"

Interviewed by the *New York Times* about his relationship with his adoptive parents after he found his birth father, Bill Wattendorf said of his adoptive parents, "When I was searching, they tried really hard to be supportive. But one time my father let out: 'What's wrong with us? Didn't we do everything for you?'"[2]

College professor Mary A. said she has never told her adoptive parents about tracking down her birth mother, even though she had hoped to introduce the subject by putting stories about people who searched in front of them as conversation starters.

"My dad said, 'That's nice,' and changed the subject. My mother said, 'If you ever search, don't tell me.' I always got strong vibes that this wasn't something I was supposed to talk about."

Newer adoptive parents, who now are more keenly aware of adoptees' need for biological roots than were those during my era, generally live with the reality of an eventual reunion in their children's futures.

Public relations and advertising executive Page Hanes, adoptive mother of two preschoolers, said she believes that adoptive parents have "an extra layer of love for their children because of the time you waited for them," and that in itself may be what causes adoptive parents initially to have ambivalent feelings about envisioning their children meeting their birth families some day. The specter of infertility—which has seen them prodded and poked by testing and procedures and then analyzed and scrutinized by agency placement interviews—can leave adoptive parents feeling physically and emotionally bruised. Then to add insult to the injury they feel, often well-meaning acquaintances badger them with questions like, "Why couldn't you two have children?" or "Was it your fault or your husband's?" Such questions add to their sense that there's something terribly wrong with them because they cannot produce a child of their own. Sometimes adoptive parents initially may regard their children's desire to know their birth families as a slap in the face at the

> *Sometimes adoptive parents initially regard their children's desire to know their birth families as a slap in the face after the've reared the child that some other family was unable to.*

devotion they've given them after they've reared the child that some other family was unable to.

Hanes attests to this dilemma and yet describes how the adoptive parents' love for the child prevails in a desire for that child's wholeness. "Part of you wishes those children were totally your own—wishes that they were your birth children and that there was not another birth father or birth mother, and wishes you could hold them to you forever. But because you love them so much you know that you will do what is best for them, and that is to give them their heritage."

"I'd Go Tomorrow"

Editorial assistant Christy Haines said she will encourage her two daughters, whom she and her husband Paul adopted as teen-agers, eventually to look up some of their birth family even though both girls were from troubled family situations.

"It will be difficult to do, but we will try to build up their self-esteem to the point that they can meet these relatives and feel good about themselves," she said. "A time will come in their lives that they'll need to do this to put their past behind them."

Although acknowledging the emotional pull of uttering such words, publicist Bracey Campbell said that if he had the opportunity to meet the birthparents of daughter Jenna, eight, "I'd go tomorrow to meet them. As loving a child as Jenna is, I'd just expect that she'd feel some attachment to her birth mother. I wouldn't fight it at all. I think this is an example of how God can take a difficult thing [such as an unplanned pregnancy] and turn it into a wonderful thing. I'd like for her birth mother to see that."

"I've prayed from the first that her birthparents would have a peace about it," said Bracey's wife, Gay. "I'd just like to be able to let them know what a wonderful little girl she is."

Using This Chapter

Adopted Persons

❊ Do not fear a conversation with your adoptive parents about your birth origins. Sometimes adoptive parents are waiting for opportunities to pass on information to you or to give you their blessing. Sometimes you and your adoptive parents have fears that need to be addressed.

❊ Let someone else's words help you broach the subject, if necessary. Use newspaper or magazine stories as a springboard for introducing the topic. Share this book with your parents. Introduce them to certain passages if you think the entire book might overwhelm them.

❊ At all times assure them of your love for them. Make the covert overt. Tell them you realize that they may be thinking that your desire to know about your birth heritage may make them wonder whether they have done something wrong as parents.

❊ Assure them of your deep, abiding appreciation for all that they are to you. Give them practical illustrations of times, such as doctor's office appointments, when you've needed to know information from your past.

❊ Pray for your adoptive parents. Thank God for them and ask Him to help you communicate love and concern to them in the process. Pray for your birth family, asking God to direct you to them and to prepare them for the time when you may make contact.

Adoptive Parents

❊ Consider whether your adoptive children may have curiosity even though they have never asked. You may need to be the ones to introduce the subject to them.

The same advice for adopted persons about sharing books and articles applies; these vehicles provide bridges to help awkward conversational waters.

❧ Understand the adopted child's need to know for medical and emotional reasons. Believe that enabling adopted persons in a search is one of the most loving gifts you can provide. Don't take it as a personal affront that you've failed or didn't provide enough. Look on it as the crown jewel of everything that you've provided for them so far.

❧ Don't be surprised if you find that you have mixed feelings when you discover your children's interest in knowing about their birth parents. Many adoptive parents find themselves initially hurt and angry, as all the hurts and dashed hopes of their struggle with infertility flood into the memory. Adoptive parents sometimes feel that all they have done for the child is being demeaned and that they'll be displaced in the child's mind. However, most eventually realize that their relationship is usually strong enough to withstand the strain of a search.

❧ Provide vital emotional support. This is a time when one of your children's greatest fears is that they will hurt the parents they love.

❧ Attend the meeting of an adopted persons' search group. Many adoptive parents say that hearing adoptees share their stories gives them a whole new perspective on why an adopted child might initiate a reunion with a birth parent.

❧ Pray that God will give you an open mind and heart and that He will show you the way you can best help your child who wants to initiate a search. Pray for your child's birth family members and that they will respond in a way that is in everyone's best interest.

Birth Parents

❧ Be aware of the reality that your birth child may contact you. Determine what your response may be. If your spouse or children don't know about your past, tell them now to give them time to react before a search might end up at your doorstep.

❧ Understand the birth child's need for information. Attend a meeting of an adopted persons' search group if you want to gain perspective on why these individuals believe they have needs.

❧ Respect the adoptive family's/adoptee's boundaries if you're the one initiating the search. Consider the adoptive parents' feelings. Try to empathize with the pain they can feel in the process.

F   O   U   R

The Search:
Whom You Might Find

❧

Once *reason at last returned to me* after I joyfully
discovered that my parents would support me in a search, I
turned my attentions to the next step—the mechanics of the
whole process. I had to think fast, because the three-day
weekend that Louis, Matthew, and I were on to visit my
parents in Garland was almost over. Any steps I took would
be twice as difficult once I returned to Houston and left the
place where some shreds of information might remain.

I decided to use the last day of my visit—a Monday—to
make my long-postponed trip to see the doctor who assisted
in the adoption plan. Mother volunteered to go with me so
we could present a united front. My birth mother's last-
known address, names of relatives, and other points of reference all might be contained in his thirty-year-old files.

At this point, new fear gripped me. The medical profession
at that time was known to be generally unreceptive to adult
adoptees. Florence Fisher, who founded the national ALMA
organization after a long search for her birth family, had the

door closed in her face when she tried to query her placing physician. Countless other adoptees heard the "You-should-be-grateful" lectures and ran into brick walls when they consulted doctors for information.

Even though my mother would be present as a show of support during this visit to the doctor, I wasn't sure how effective she would be against such an attitude.

The night before our appointment with the doctor, I geared for battle. After reporting on the adoptee rights movement for several years, I knew all the arguments and felt I could counter any resistant statement the doctor might make. Louis and I stayed up half the night role-playing, with him tossing me the doctor's potential barbs.

Assuming the Worst

Adoptees like myself had become used to the warning, "You'll never know who you might find," which was always stated quite dramatically. It was as though people automatically assumed birth mothers to be people on skid row or death row or worse. Although I knew it was possible that I might find birth family living in unfortunate circumstances, I remembered that Marty Renault's mother Winnie certainly wasn't someone whose life had taken a bad turn. After Marty was born and adopted, Winnie worked in a bank, eventually married and reared three children, and was living with her husband in a comfortable home south of Houston. And other birth mothers I had written about in reunion stories were just average people—not people who stood out in a crowd as having had this experience. They merely were women who at some point in the past had made a choice or had a circumstance in their lives from which there was a very obvious consequence. If the doctor hurled the "You-never-know-whom-you-might-find" caveat at me, I was prepared to answer, "The important thing to an adoptee is not who you find but that you find something."

In the end, I was girded for a battle that I never had to fight. The doctor, a longtime friend of my parents in their community, welcomed us warmly. At first he scratched his head when I asked him if he could remember the circumstances of my adoption. So many babies were placed back then, he said. It was difficult to isolate just one in his memory.

But when I supplied details such as my birthdate and other pertinent time frames, a smile of recognition crossed his face. "Ah, yes, 1948," he pondered. "That was when Jean was my nurse. Well, since that's the case, then I do remember your story." And out poured the cherished details.

My birth mother was a friend of his former nurse, he recalled. Nurse Jean had arranged for Eleanor to come to Texas so that her child could be born in a place remote from her hometown. She had lived with Jean and her parents in Garland until it came time for her delivery date. After that, Eleanor returned to her native state to start a new life.

Perhaps his former nurse, who since had moved away but who still sent him Christmas cards, would know how to reach my birth mother, the doctor ventured. He gave me the nurse's address and his sincere best wishes. I was speechless with relief and gratitude.

Much Soul-Searching

I now had the name of the person who was the one remaining link between me and the missing person in my life. At that point, I had to do much soul-searching and praying. ALMA had some definite guidelines for appropriate reunion ethics.

Intermediaries, like the nurse would be, definitely were not a part of ALMA's game plan. ALMA founder Florence Fisher cautioned adopted persons not to use a go-between when a search was under way. Intermediaries, she believed, only would muddy the waters. In one case she cited, both an adoptee and a birth mother had told the same social worker that they wished to be united. But the worker never relayed the message to either person. Florence believed that the adopted person must do his or her own legwork, even if that meant a longer search.

But patience never was one of my attributes. The idea of tracking Eleanor down through city directories, marriage licenses, and other public records—the only route some adoptees had when searching for parents—seemed ridiculous when I had an easier way.

> *I prepared so many notes, one would think I were getting ready to argue a case before the Supreme Court.*

More importantly, through an intermediary, Eleanor would have an option of saying no. If she told the nurse that my appearing on the scene would cause her problems with a present husband or children, I could back off quietly and wait for another time. It seemed the only considerate, nonintrusive thing to do.

So, before I called the nurse, I again geared for battle—this time on a fuller scale than before. I prepared so many notes, one would think I were getting ready to argue a case before the Supreme Court.

My four pages of single-spaced notes had statistics I scavenged from *The Adoption Triangle*, the trailblazing book on the effects of sealed records on adopted persons, birthparents, and adoptive parents. This landmark material had estimates about the high number of birth mothers believed to be open to reunions. It claimed that "the adoptee, ignorant of his/her true background despite a healthy nurturing relationship with his/her adoptive parents, will be handicapped in the psychohistorical dimensions of identity."[1] I could cite quotes from social workers about adoptees' psychological needs. I could out talk anyone, anywhere on the subject.

Engineering the Contact

But again, the battle I expected to fight never occurred. The nurse had received a letter from the Garland doctor earlier in the week and was expecting my call.

"I'm not looking for another family," I explained to her on the phone. "I have plenty of family already. And I'm not trying to disrupt my birth mother's life. I don't want to barge in on her and her family. But there are some things about my biological past that only she can tell me. Do you think she is willing?"

The nurse responded she hadn't seen Eleanor in about twenty years but said she thought she could engineer the contact. I was to call the nurse back in a few days.

But when the moment of truth arrived, she had good news and bad news. My birth mother, who lived in Colorado, would talk to me, reported the nurse. Her husband, who had known about my existence all along, was willing. So was her grown daughter (what a thrill to know I had a half-sister!!) who had not known about these past incidents but who had accepted the news with aplomb.

Even more amazing, the nurse said, was the news that I was a journalist.

"There are three generations of journalists in her family," the nurse reported. "Both her grandfathers were newspaper editors; her mother still writes a column for a small-town paper, and Eleanor herself was a journalism student in college."

But one real snag existed in the whole new turn of events, the nurse went on to say. "Eleanor's mother has just had a heart attack and is not expected to live," she said.

"Things are under a real strain there." She gave me the long-awaited telephone number of Eleanor's home but did so with the warning, "I wouldn't call right now if I were you."

My heart sank as I bemoaned being so near and yet so far. With horror, I imagined myself placing the crucial phone call in the midst of funeral preparations.

How boorish I would seem! I never realized how tricky timing was in this whole delicate process. I feared that one wrong move could undermine much careful strategy.

No More Waiting

One, two, three, four, five days passed, as the slip of paper containing the phone number grew hotter in my hand. At the end of the week, I would be leaving for the ALMA conference. I would be a nervous wreck while I covered the meeting if I knew that some very unfinished business hung over my head.

By the fifth night, I knew I could wait no more. My nerves were frayed, and my patience was worn thin. After Louis and I put Matthew to bed, Louis placed the call, for a very specific reason. Eleanor's husband and daughter, who lived at home, by now were obviously aware of my interest. If one of them answered, they might recognize that the call was long-distance, but a male voice would throw them. I didn't want things to foul up at this stage of the game.

I heard for the first time the voice of the woman who gave me physical life.

A few rings, and then success. Louis smiled a big smile. "Is Eleanor there? Okay, would you hold on just a minute?"

So within the next few moments, I heard for the first time the voice of the woman who gave me physical life.

What do you say to a mother whom you have never seen? Many people have asked in the years since. The answer is really quite simple. You converse just as you do with any stranger whom you seek to know better. At first the conversation was general, as we exchanged current information about occupations (she had been a first-grade school teacher for thirty years and had never worked as a journalist although she was trained to be one), family size, and interests.

My question, "What do you look like?" brought answers to years of frustration. She too was short, small in build, and had dark hair. When I stammered, "I have to ask you something about my teeth," she replied quickly, "Are you missing some permanent ones, too?" In that one instant I bridged the gap that began in the dentist's chair when I was eight.

Her family was predominantly of German and Dutch descent, with some French and English blood also. This information voided the poll of my college chums which made me an honorary Italian.

God's Good Timing

And no, her mother had not died during the week. In fact, her condition was better. She might be going home soon. So my contact hadn't blown matters apart after all. And I marveled at God's good timing and thanked Him for giving me patience to wait until a brighter day to place the call.

Then, at last, we moved to more important matters. My birth father was a fellow college student who declined to marry her when she told him about her pregnancy. Although she had not seen him in years, she knew his current whereabouts. "Call him up sometime; it would serve him right," she quipped.

As time grew nearer for the birth, her nurse friend invited her to move from Colorado to Garland, where they lived with her friend's parents. As I knew already, that nurse worked for the doctor who helped make the adoption plan for me.

As was common practice for the time, my birth mother never saw or held the child she gave birth to but was told only of my gender and physical description at birth. Shortly afterward, she returned home to try to put the developments of the previous nine months out of her mind.

After nearly an hour of conversation, we parted, each promising to write and hopefully meet some day. For the remainder of the evening, I moved as though in a dream. I realized that it would take weeks, even months or years, for the whole impact of that conversation to be truly felt.

Now, I had a past as well as a future.

But from the first, one emotion stood out above all the rest. As of that night, I was no longer a dandelion. I once sentimentally compared myself to the dandelion's fuzz ball because it seemed that my life might be here today, gone tomorrow, without being linked to the generations of the past.

But now, I had a past as well as a future. Not only would my heritage extend forward in time through Matthew and any other children I might have, it also went back in time, through Eleanor and her forebears. And for an adoptee, that knowledge was dynamite.

A Fifteen-Year Search

If the search for my birth family was simple and tidy, Linda Sledge's was just the opposite and at times boiled down to nothing short of detective work on her part. It began at the Fort Worth adoption agency where she saw the actual bassinet where she had lain twenty-six years before when her adoptive parents came to take her home. It ended seventeen years later in a Houston high school library where she found her birth mother's photo in an album.

Although her visit to the agency yielded little information, an attorney friend was later able to retrieve her file from a judge on the condition that the attorney would agree to use a social worker/investigator appointed by his court. The social worker looked in the file and contacted Linda's birth mother, who said she was unwilling to have Linda make contact.

Undaunted by this refusal, Linda continued to pursue leads to see if she could meet some of her birth mother's family even if her birth mother didn't feel comfortable meeting her. This time she petitioned for her records and was able to get them released to her; however, all the identifying information was whited out.

"I could see that the name of the high school that she attended was different from the name of the town where she lived because one of the names had a letter with a tail [descender] on it while the other one didn't. In 1949 only two towns in Texas were large enough to have more than one high school. By the process of elimination I knew that it was Houston"—the city where Linda lived as an adult. "I also by process of elimination could figure out which high school it was since Reagan High School was the only one of the older schools in town that contained six letters in its name," she said.

By this point Linda had learned from the social worker her birth mother's first name, and had learned from the whited-out document her birth mother's age at the time of her birth. Linda and a longtime friend then visited the high school library and looked through old annuals. "I knew from the information the social worker gave me that my birth mother, who was a high-school junior, had a brother a year younger than she was. So I looked in the annual and found a junior student who had a younger brother who was a sophomore. The girl's picture resembled me a great deal. Her first and last name had the same number of characters that the whited-out name had in the document. I knew then that I had found my family."

Now that she knew a last name, Linda continued her search by looking through the Houston city directory for that year under her birth mother's family name. By calling the telephone number in the city directory, she determined that her birth grandmother still lived at that same address but was in the hospital. Not wanting to intrude on the sick, elderly woman, Linda persuaded a nurse in her church to call the hospital and obtain the name of her grandmother's next-of-kin. Through this connection Linda learned that her birth mother had a sister who was only two years older than Linda. She sent this sister—her aunt—a letter and picture and adoption records. A week after her aunt received the letter, she and Linda met, giving Linda her first link with biological kin.

"This woman had no idea that I existed, but she saw all the information that I had and saw that the pieces fit and believed me," she said. "She then told her brother—my uncle, the one who was a year younger than my mother. He was aware of the story from many years ago and absolutely confirmed all the events in my birth mother's life that I had pieced together."

A Way to Explain Things

Kristen Cunningham's finding her birth family came from an opposite kind of experience—her birth mother's search for her. Although it reflected the more open approach to adoptee-birth mother relations in the 1980s, it was no less suspense-filled and gratifying than for people whose cases for years were shrouded in mystery.

When Kristen was a college freshman, her adoptive mother made her aware that her birth mother, Wendy, had contacted her placing agency and notified it that she desired contact with the daughter she made an adoption plan for eighteen years before.

"The agency actually had contacted my mother when I was fourteen and notified her that my birth mother was interested in meeting me someday, but my mother wisely kept this information from me until I was ready. We had just moved to a new town and I had started a new high school, and I was too young for that then," said Kristen.

When she entered college, however, Kristen's parents told her about her birth mother's desire for contact and gave

Kristen their full blessing. She prayed for direction and felt God telling her to proceed. "In the fall of my sophomore year I wrote her for the first time, and she wrote back, sending lots of photos. We began writing every two months or so. Her tone matched my tone; we were proceeding cautiously."

Although letters arrived frequently, Kristen and Wendy didn't know each other's last names for more than two years. "We finally wrote the agency and asked if we could know last names so that we could write each other directly instead of having to use the agency as the intermediary," Kristen said. The agency consented, and the two women were able to finally correspond under their complete identities.

It's just a lot of helpful stuff to know.

"I held off sending a grown-up photo of me and sent her only pictures from my childhood at first," said Kristen. "I wanted her to wait and see me in person if we ever did meet." But Kristen soon grew impatient and sent Wendy a current photo.

Kristen said the best part of knowing her birth family was "having someone I could direct my questions to. There were some things about me, like my laid-back temperament in a family of type-A personalities, that I couldn't explain. But I was able to learn from Wendy that my birth father (whom Wendy dated but did not marry) was just like this. Wendy and I have the same gaps in our front teeth. And Wendy and I both are in helping professions. It's just a lot of helpful stuff to know."

More Than Just Facts

Tana Hill, who as an infant was adopted through a state agency, applied to the state to receive her medical history and then decided she wanted more than just facts. By paying a fee, she placed her name on a registry, where her birth mother had left her name five years earlier, indicating she would be willing to have contact with the daughter for whom she made an adoption plan. When Tana listed her name, the connection was immediate. Her birth mother and family lived less than an hour away from Tana. Immediately she learned that her birth grandmother sang in a musical group, thus helping explain Tana's musical abilities that she had wondered about since childhood, and that she has the same cheekbones and brown eyes.

College professor Mary A. learned the name of her birth mother by writing directly to the hospital where she knew she was born. To her surprise, the hospital sent her the name and address of her birth mother. With that information she hired a professional search consultant in California. Six months later the consultant found her birth mother. Even though her grandmother told her that her birth mother was from "out East," her birth mother actually was born in a Midwestern town not too far from where Mary was born and had grown up in the town where Mary went to college.

She said she wanted to meet her birth mother to see if she could track down the root of certain dissimilarities from her adoptive family. "I learned to read [avidly] when I was very young, and my mother always said, 'You didn't get that from your dad or me.' I wrote stories incessantly, and no one felt about animals the way that I did. I just wanted to know someone who thought like I thought."

A social worker employed by the state helped hospital marketing specialist Jacqueline Jagger track down her birth mother after Jacqueline contacted the state for help. Jacqueline's second child was born with a heart defect, and during her third pregnancy Jacqueline appealed to the state to learn medical information. The social worker agreed to arrange the reunion after Jacqueline's birth mother consented.

"We found some musical abilities and some writing abilities in common," said Jacqueline. "I was relieved that she had told her husband about me before they were married. I didn't want to be the skeleton in someone's closet. That's a tough one to dance in front of someone, so I was grateful he knew. Their two [college-age] girls didn't know. She called them in and said, 'Twenty-six years ago, I made a mistake.' They didn't respond: 'Oh, how awful.' They said, 'Where is she? When can we meet her?' It made the whole thing much easier."

Locating her birth mother was no difficulty for social worker Carolyn Wells, who was adopted by an aunt when her birth mother's marriage fell apart and her mother moved. Carolyn grew up knowing the true identity of her birth mother and even saw her on rare occasions.

But "finding" her birth mother in the true sense had to wait until the woman who reared her died because "there was much jealousy there" between her birth mother and the aunt who reared her. Only after what Carolyn calls their "reuniting experience" was Carolyn able to talk with her mother about "what her life was really like" during those days when she relinquished her child to be reared by a sister. "She felt very hopeless and helpless, and I was at last able to hear her story," Carolyn says.

Painful Yet Productive

Knowing that he doubtless would uncover painful circumstances did not deter freelance writer Joe Wilson from tracking down his birth parents, from whom the state removed him and four other siblings when he was six. Joe and his sister and brothers were sent to foster homes after a court declared them neglected children. Joe was adopted four years later and was reared without knowing anything about his parents other than his own dim memories.

When Joe was thirty-four, one of his siblings from whom he was separated located him. He and his sister then looked up their birth mother and birth father, who were divorced.

Even though his birth mother—who eventually remarried, reared a family, and was retired—expressed no remorse about what had happened to her children, Joe was gratified he met her. "You feel like you're floating on an iceberg—disconnected from the main continent," he said about the limbo stage of not knowing his birth family.

The need for a birth certificate so she could obtain a passport for foreign business travel launched administrative assistant Betsy DeShano into a search that uncovered grisly facts yet answered some major questions on the part of Betsy and her family members. Adopted at age five and reared believing that her parents were killed in a car accident, Betsy applied to the state for her original certificate. In turn, she discovered two birth sisters who along with Betsy were removed from their birthhome when their father murdered their mother. As the three girls then tried to connect with a maternal birth grandmother, they learned of her whereabouts but saw that she had no phone and was listed only with a box number. Betsy's husband Phillip made repeated calls to a general store in the area to ask if anyone who might be in the store knew Betsy's birth grandmother. After calling the store every day for two weeks, Phillip achieved success when a small girl who was shopping in the store heard Betsy's grandmother's name called out and said she was a relative of hers. The little girl then helped Betsy connect with Betsy's birth grandmother, who pieced together for Betsy the story of her mother's murder.

> *The important thing to an adoptee is not who you find but that you find something.*

Fear of her father, who had been convicted of the murder, and the need to know his whereabouts for her own protection propelled Betsy to search further rather than to stop. When she did connect with her father's brother, she "couldn't believe he was such a wonderful man." He explained that her father, who had suffered from severe depression and was an alcoholic, committed suicide after being released from prison, straightening out his life, and then falling back into depression again. She learned that her father's family had been large landowners and that her father had been a wealthy man but had squandered his money on alcohol. "It was horrible information, but it put things into perspective and relieved all our fears," she said. "It gave me peace I needed so I could get on with the rest of my life."

Truly, adoptees who search with a passion bear witness the claim that I had been prepared to make at the doctor's office: The important thing to an adoptee is not who you find but that you find something.

Using This Chapter

Adopted Persons

❦ Realize that no two searches are alike. Some occur as neatly as clockwork; others take years of frustration. Don't enter a search expecting it will be easy—or inexpensive. Even without fees for professional searchers, the cost of calls, gasoline, and/or plane fares can add up quickly.

❦ Be prepared for any kind of scenario to unfold. Some people find that their records have been falsified; others find that expected barriers to their information actually do not exist.

❦ Understand that the very best source for your birth family information is your adoptive parents. They are more likely to know the information that either will fill in the gaps or put you on the proper trail to search. Don't hesitate to bring up the subject with them and see what information you can obtain, even if you fear a negative reaction. You might be pleasantly surprised.

❦ Respect the birth family's privacy. Consider asking a third party to be a contact person. If calling directly, make contacts at times when other family members are not likely to be present until you are certain everyone in the family knows.

✻ Enlist someone to help you roleplay. This can prepare you for various types of developments in your search.

✻ Be respectful of what life events might be going on in your birth family at the time of contact. While some birth mothers wait all their lives for such a moment, others have not thought about what might happen if they are found and still others, although a minority, object to a reunion.

Adoptive Parents

✻ Rear children with much love and self-esteem. Then they can deal with whatever is in their background.

✻ Don't presume that because your children came from difficult backgrounds, that they are not strong enough to search—or that birthparents would reject them.

✻ Encourage children to build a strong relationships with the heavenly Father. This is the best foundation for any life experience.

Birth Parents

✻ Realize that many adopted persons are satisfied simply to see or talk with the birth parents and gather information. Many do not push for actual contact.

✻ Be aware that most adopted persons sincerely desire to treat such situations with respect. Let the adopted person know right away your concerns and boundaries.

✻ Keep the setting of a reunion natural. Adopted persons want to see how you live and understand your frame of reference, not be entertained. A neutral setting, like a hotel lobby or an airport, sometimes works best for a reunion because one party will not have an edge over the other one in terms of familiar circumstances.

The Reunion:
The End of the Jetway

🌿

So with all these events at last behind me—the wondering, the soul-searching, the strategizing, the researching, the explaining, the praying—I took a deep breath, clutched my box of roses for support, and walked into the by-now almost vacant airport waiting room, where I saw the figures of three people clustered at the edge of the gate. A few feet closer, I realized to my relief that spotting the party waiting for me would be no problem as I feared. The smallest of the three took a few steps forward, and held out her arms, and there was instant recognition.

Words do not exist to describe—even to my husband and parents later—that high and intensely personal moment when I first laid eyes on my birth mother. But when speech finally returned after the initial hugs and squeals, I handed Eleanor the flower box and explained the event of my childhood that happened every Mother's Day and that involved the white rose.

"Since you're obviously alive, I decided to wear a red rose today," I said. "And I wanted you to have some, too."

Besides the joy of meeting Eleanor and her understanding husband Charles—who at one point pulled me aside and confided, "I've been wanting this to happen for years"—I had the added thrill of getting to know my half-sister, who was tall, statuesque, regal, and had little resemblance to me except for one feature—the same missing permanent teeth, a fact that I obviously took delight in knowing. Coincidentally, her name was Catharine, the name Louis and I had picked for a daughter before our son Matthew was born (and we did, of course, eventually name our second child two years later). As we became acquainted, I found that she was the kind of person I would have enjoyed knowing even if we were not blood kin.

Catching Up on History

The weekend passed with the three of us women asking and answering inane questions like: "Did you ever have bone spurs?" "Are you terribly near-sighted, too?" And "How about varicose veins?" Time seemed to stand still as I basked in the answers to thirty years of wondering.

And the photo albums! As I viewed hundreds of old family photographs and saw my nose in one picture, my eyes in another, I felt a heretofore unknown physical connection with past generations.

We spent time driving around to various nostalgic spots in town, such as the house where Eleanor was born, the neighborhood where she grew up, and the schools she attended. Her family tried to incorporate me very casually into the activities they most enjoyed, such as sailboating, and I felt very much one with them from the start.

On the last night of my trip, my newfound sister cooked and served a special candlelight dinner to celebrate my visit. To my delight, the family invited the nurse who had helped me find Eleanor only a few weeks ago and to whom I was so indebted.

It was Eleanor's husband Charles who opened a college yearbook and who showed me a picture of my birth father. With that, the final gap was closed. Perhaps someday, after I assimilated all the events of the past few weeks, I would be ready to track him down, too. After all, I was still curious about the "always familial" tiny white moles my dermatologist removed year after year, which turned out not to be a trait of Eleanor's family.

Meeting Extended Kin

During that weekend, as Eleanor introduced me to various relatives and friends, I let her set the pace in terms of exactly how much information she chose to provide each person we met. To her older brother—my uncle by birth—with whom we visited at the airport as my plane was about to depart, no details were held back. I was presented as the daughter for whom Eleanor had made an adoption plan years ago. Her brother, well aware of the long-ago circumstances, was gracious and accepting of my visit.

However, to other relatives who may not have known the details of that period when Eleanor left Colorado for a time when she was a young woman, I merely was introduced as "Kay, a friend visiting us from Texas." And the same set of guidelines applied when I met her mother—my birth grandmother, whose small, wiry frame I immediately recognized as being like my own. Because of her recent illness, and undoubtedly because the events of my birth had caused a strain in the family at that time, Eleanor chose not to reveal to her my exact identity. As Eleanor and I sat side by side as mirror images of one another on the sofa at her mother's home, however, it seemed that no one could actually have missed the uncanny resemblance. During that visit, I had an almost uncontrollable urge to reach out and hug this frail, reserved woman and say,

"Don't you see? Everything turned out okay. You may not have known me all these years, but you can be proud of me now." I thought about my own dear grandmothers, now deceased, and my Bandad, whose passing three years before had left a huge hole in my life. How much I did, at thirty, still have a longing to be someone's special grandchild—someone to be doted on, someone to be adored! I prayed that this tiny, taciturn lady would, as Gay Campbell said about her daughter's birth mother, someday have a peace about those long-ago events, even if I never had the privilege of meeting her under my true identity.

Lowering Expectations

These sentiments were shared by Linda Sledge, whose birth grandmother learned of Linda's desire to meet her but who died without choosing to grant Linda's wish. Linda said this turn of events almost was more difficult for her to accept than when her birth mother declined to make contact.

"I had all these expectations," Linda said. "In my childhood I always believed that I had a [birth] grandmother who was praying for me and who was anxious to know how I'd turned out. It was hard for me to realize that when she had the opportunity, she made that choice. I wanted my [teen-age] sons to meet her. They had a hard time understanding it, too. They said, 'What's wrong with us? We're neat folks. Why shouldn't anyone like us?' And our family actually lived about ten minutes away from my grandmother's home. We could have helped with her care and shared part of that burden. I hope that just the fact of knowing what little she did about me gave her some peace before she passed away."

Linda said she was consoled by the enjoyment she has knowing her aunt and uncle, her two birth family members who have been open to a reunion with Linda and her family. "I'm thankful that I've been able to get as much information as I have from them," she said. "It's especially nice knowing my aunt, who seems more like a sister because she's so near my age."

In accepting Eleanor's decision, I too had to thank God for the birth family contacts that were available to me, believing that at least for the time being, decisions about such matters were Eleanor's call. I also realized that I already knew more about my birth family than some searching adopted persons ever would. I had massive respect for Eleanor for being willing to open her life to me to the degree that she had. To be an established adult with a career and standing in your community and neighborhood—and then to suddenly be in the position of presenting a child you bore in your youth and did not rear was more than many people could tolerate. As time arrived for this poignant visit to Colorado to end, I was awestruck with what I had accomplished. In my last few minutes with this newfound family, I found myself soaking up similarities as though I were cramming for an exam. I wanted to imprint her features indelibly in my mind in case I had no more visits to look back on.

> *In my last few minutes with this newfound family, I found myself soaking up similarities as though I were cramming for an exam. I wanted to imprint her features indelibly in my mind in case I had no more visits to look back on.*

A Tough Parting

Kristen Cunningham describes having the same type of emotion when she met her birth mother, Wendy. "I hadn't slept the whole night before," says Kristen, who finally met Wendy after she and husband Grant had been married for a few years and were out on their own. Grant and Kristen's parents were both by Kristen's side during the meeting in an airport.

"I just wanted to look at her toes and fingers and hold her hands," says Kristen about seeing Wendy, with whom she had corresponded for three years by that time. "I would find myself staring at her and then having to look away because I didn't want to seem rude."

Although much of the reunion time was spent in a group experience, Kristen and Wendy finally were able to spend some time alone. "Wendy was relieved to know that there was no bitterness on my part. And I was glad to know that things had gone so well in her life."

When Kristen out of courtesy refrained from asking about her birth father, Wendy finally volunteered, "Well, don't you want to know about your father?" Wendy then told her what she knew about the young man whom she had dated for two years but had not married. Both Wendy and Kristen's birth father, Donnie, eventually married other people, and Wendy now was a single mother of two.

> *Many birth mothers describe the reunion experience as akin to bonding between mother and baby at the start of life, so it's no wonder that saying goodbye after the first meeting brings fresh grief.*

"When we parted, we both cried and cried," recalls Kristen. "It was like separating all over again. It was interesting that we felt this way even though we had known each other for three years." Many birth mothers describe the reunion experience as being akin to the bonding between mother and baby at the start of life, so it's no wonder that saying goodbye after the first meeting brings fresh grief.

Instead of driving a wedge, as Kristen had feared, the experience caused her to grow closer to her adoptive parents. She said, "Just going through it with them and knowing they supported me meant a lot. It was especially rewarding to have them there at the airport with me that day."

Jacqueline Jagger said of her reunion with her birth mother in a Texas hotel: "We drove up to the hotel, I walked in the lobby, and there I was, staring me in the face. Our eyes were the same—and our hip structure! At first the meeting was a little bit strained. I had questions like, 'What do these people expect of me, and what do I expect of them?' But then it grew very warm."

Tana Hill, who learned after connecting through the state's registry that she lived less than an hour away from her birth mother, "called her up, and we met the same night." Besides meeting her mother, Tana was greeted by a full sister, born two years after Tana while her mother remained unmarried to their father, and two half sisters. The sisters "had always known about me," Tana said. "She had always told them that I was around. It opened a whole new world for me."

Betsy DeShano's reunion with her birth family was a tremendous relief for her birth grandmother, who had kept up with Betsy when she lived in various foster homes but who had lost track of the child after she was adopted at age five. Although her mother's family had wanted to adopt Betsy and her sisters after the family tragedy when her mother was murdered, her grandmother was unable to do so because of economic circumstances.

When Betsy and her husband Phillip drove up to her grandmother's rural home and met the woman for the first time, "She hugged me like I've never been hugged before," Betsy said. From the grandmother, she learned that her mother died with her body covering tiny Betsy, who was three months old at the time. "I always wondered if I was loved, and I found out that my mother may have died while trying to protect me,'" she said.

Joe Wilson said he and his birth mother "talked about the weather" during their inconsequential conversation on their first meeting. But during a later visit, when he and his birth mother went for a drive, "She spilled her guts. She told me how she liked to go out dancing and drinking and to have fun. The judge told her that she would lose her kids if she continued. She saw it as a challenge—she thought, 'He won't do that. He's just throwing his weight around.' But he did. It helped to at last hear the story."

Joe said one of the most helpful parts of their meeting occurred when his birth mother showed him where he was born. "I was born in a doctor's office because the town didn't have hospitals. It's a parking lot now because the building was torn down, but it meant a lot to me to see it. Since I hadn't grown up in my family, I had no one to keep memories alive for me. I enjoyed having them recreated."

Unlike his birth mother, Joe's birth father "has never offered any kind of explanation. He refers all questions to my birth mother." Despite this, Joe says he is grateful to know his birth father. "I see a lot of my mannerisms in my dad," he says. "We both talk too fast sometimes, and he's kind of nervous. It's like seeing how I'll be thirty years from now."

Joe says he didn't tell his adoptive parents about his search until after he met his birth parents. His adoptive mother "is bothered" by his searching, but Joe says his father "kinda expected it."

The Other Shoe to Drop

Like Kristen Cunningham and Joe as they processed their visits, I was concerned about how my visit to Colorado would impact my relationship with my parents. Once back home after my glorious trip, the old worries returned to plague me just once more. I wondered how my parents would react now that the meeting was accomplished. Would this new family, so dear to me after only one meeting, be viewed as a threat by the only family I had known for years? I somehow felt I was waiting for the other shoe to drop.

But a short note from my mother a few days after my trip put all the worries to rest for keeps.

"Dear Kay," it read, "We're so happy about your trip. If I could express myself the way you can, I'd write Eleanor and tell her thanks for giving a couple of 'senior citizens' the chance to rear a precious individual like you. We're truly glad that you have found each other." She said she and Daddy couldn't wait to meet Charles and Eleanor and hoped they would have the opportunity some day.

"I knew if I didn't have her love after these thirty years, I wouldn't have it at all," my mother told a friend some days after my *Chronicle* series ran and friends began to query her about the reunion. "You have to let go sometime."

Only a few days later, I had my first chance to try out some of my new knowledge, and I felt the circle was complete.

During an interview with a local Hispanic judge, I copied down a phrase he recited. As I repeated it for him to check for accuracy, I gave the Spanish words an accent in French, the only foreign language I speak.

"You said that in French," the judge instantly remarked. "You must be French. You look it."

At that I pounded my fist down so sharply on the desk that it must have startled the poor judge.

"I'm German and Dutch," I exclaimed, with a huge grin.

And this time, as never before, I knew the triumph of speaking the truth.

Using This Chapter

Adopted Persons

🌿 Let the birth family set the pace for the reunion visits. Be understanding and patient if they don't desire to go public with everything immediately. This may change over time.

❦ A birth family member's refusal to meet you does not reflect on your self-worth. It may reflect on how that family dealt with the adoption originally or that person's willingness to be open about a difficult time in his or her life. Remember that a birth parent not only has to face how he or she felt about losing you but also how he or she felt about losing the relationship with the other birth parent, if that occurred. Your arrival into a birth parent's life may be a fresh reminder of a failed or disappointing or deceptive relationship that brought heartache. Be understanding as your birth parent deals with those feelings.

❦ Be thankful for what information you are able to obtain and recognize the immense courage on the birth parent's part to open this part of his or her life to you, even if it is only a tiny bit. Pray that God will use whatever contact you have with your birth parent to help ease his or her pain and your need.

❦ After a reunion, try to avoid painting to your adoptive parents a picture of a birth mother or birth father who "can do no wrong." Adoptive parents often secretly feel concerned that their child will meet a birth parent who has none of their imperfections and therefore will be put on a pedestal far beyond what the adoptive parents can attain. They may feel that their loving and caring count for nothing in comparison to the intrigue and glamour of finding the birth family. They may feel that the birth parent is arriving late on the scene to bask in the glory of their years of blood-sweat-and-tears investment in you. Don't let your early fascination for and preoccupation with the birth parent come across to your adoptive parents as though you are making comparisons and consider them inadequate. Very few reunions result in adopted persons moving in with birth parents afterwards. Usually enough love exists to go around.

Adoptive Parents

❧ Support your adopted son or daughter unfailingly during this time. Be especially present emotionally for him or her after the first meeting with the birth family. Be available to help the adoptee process the experiences, but don't pry. Adoptees desire to feel that this was "their" experience—a real step of growth on their part. Chances are they'll want to share it with you since few other people in their lives would be interested to the degree you would. Adopted persons truly need the support of their adoptive parents to carry them through this milestone.

❧ If some aspect of the search and reunion bothers you, be honest about it. Tell your child, "I feel left out right now because you seem so absorbed in this reunion. I need your attention, too." Asking for affirmation will help remind the adopted individual to keep the event in perspective. Be careful to avoid guilt trips, however. Be specific about what kind of affirmation you need.

Birth Parents

❧ If you are a party in a search and reunion experience, you can set the boundaries about who knows how much. Take your time, and go slow. Later, after the events of the reunion have been experienced, you may decide to go more public.

❧ Provide the adopted individual as much information as you can comfortably. Adopted persons soak up every detail, even details you may think are trivial. More than likely you were reared in the family into which you were born, so you may have a difficult time understanding the adopted person's preoccupation with finding the store where you bought your first bubble gum or the sidewalk where you skinned your knee on the way home from school. Remember that people not adopted have grown up with these details and consider them unimportant, while adopted individuals consider that they've found gold when they turn up any new fact at all.

❦ Offer to give your birth child details about the other birth parent. Many times adoptees hesitate to ask for fear of bringing up a hurtful subject. If at all possible, ease this situation for your child by making those facts available without the child's having to ask.

❦ Tell your birth child feelings as well as facts. Adopted individuals often don't just want to know details about your pedigree or all the dates and times at which incidents in your life occurred; they want to know how you felt when you made an adoption plan and how you felt on their birthdays. Don't invent feelings if they aren't there, but don't try to minimize or be fearful of expressing them, either.

❦ Expect that parting after the first few meetings may be emotional because it can bring back experiences of the first loss. For many the meeting may represent the first time a birth parent, severed from the child at birth, starts to feel whole again. Be patient with yourself and don't underestimate the event's effect on you.

S I X

The Aftermath:
On Being Made in Secret

🌿

I *had thought that waiting to see* how my adoptive parents
would react in the wake of my reunion with my birth family
was tantamount to waiting for the last shoe to drop—but I
soon learned of their unfaltering love and support. Even after
that, however, I realized that anxiety gripped me about one
other matter. I was on edge about what would transpire next
regarding an ongoing relationship with the people I just met.

When we said our goodbyes at the Colorado airport after
that three-day visit, both my birth mother and I pledged to
each other that this would be more than a one-time contact.
But would it? I wondered after I returned to Texas. Although
I had tried to act casual about it, I realized how very important
it was to me that they now come visit me at my home
turf—especially to see Matthew, who would be their first
grandchild since neither my half-sister Catharine nor Charles' two children by a former marriage as yet had any children.

Some reunions I had read about lapsed into Christmas-
card relationships after the initial meeting. In those situations

all parties agreed that the information was collected, the missing puzzle pieces were found, and the drama had run its course, with no further contact desired.

> *I very much wanted to make these new loved ones a permanent part of my life.*

After only one meeting, I knew that this kind of situation was not for me. I very much wanted to make these new loved ones a permanent part of my life. Saying goodbye had been gut-wrenching because it was difficult to end something that had just begun. To never see them again would be almost as heartbreaking as never having seen them at all.

Reunion Reprise

Fortunately, I didn't have long to wait to get my wish. Within a month Charles and Eleanor had hopped on a plane and were in Houston for another unforgettable visit.

No square inch of my house was left unscrubbed; no recipe in any of my cookbooks was left untried. I planned this reunion reprise in even more detail than I meticulously mapped out the first. I wanted them never to forget the moment they looked into the face of the little boy whose dancing brown eyes, I'm convinced, were inherited from his birth grandmother. And when they met my husband of ten years, whose "Go for it!" was the glue that kept me stuck to the task of searching during many dubious days, I wanted that to be a priceless memory for them, too.

But after the glitz of the early, emotional visits of high drama settled into a more matter-of-fact routine, the great tide of exchanged facts that gushed forth in the first few contacts slowed to a less effusive stream. It was then that I began to hear Eleanor go beyond relating facts and begin uncovering feelings, as she told a story that bespoke of the embarrassment, fear, uncertainty, and self-condemnation that came from bearing a child but not rearing it.

I'll never forget the conversation when Eleanor described to me her thirty-year career of teaching first-grade in a lower-income part of her hometown. In my mind I could view Eleanor patiently drilling academically deprived youngsters until letters miraculously formed words—a skill that eventually could help lift them from their impoverished circumstances.

"There must be an awful lot of little poor children that can read and write today because of you," I suggested. Her answer to that suggestion saddens me even today.

"I paid my debt to society," she replied sternly. And that haunting remark began my realization of how women in her circumstances felt they had to almost "work off" their shame from having to make an adoption plan for a child—an earning of one's way to re-spectability—after being caught in such a predicament.

Even her vocation of schoolteaching, though honorable, was second choice. The profession of journalism, the one that I had so freely been able to enter with my B.A., was not available to

> *Countless birth parents tell about marking every birthday after making adoption plans for their children, of scanning the faces of youngsters at malls, movie theaters, fairgrounds.*

her despite four years of college training toward that goal. By the time she returned from Garland to Colorado after giving birth, going to work to support herself as a single woman on her own took first priority. With men back from World War II and filling reporter slots, no time existed to compete for a job in what clearly was then still a man's profession. Teaching, the obvious thing for women in those days to do, was a quick and logical entree to a paycheck. That's where she landed, and it stuck, but not always happily.

And did she spend those thirty intervening years pining for the child she adopted? Many birth mothers report a lifetime of craving contact with their birth child—of feeling as if they might never know whether their children are dead or alive. Winnie Ferguson described day after day of looking into crowds at every pretty girl she saw and searching for one that might have been her offspring. Blonde-haired Wendy, Kristen Cunningham's mother, became misty eyed whenever she saw a blonde child. Many speak of a nagging sense of loss as a result of the severing of this most instinctive of bonds—the bond between parent and child.

Jacqueline Jagger's birth mother Eva, related to Jacqueline that "She always had hoped to have the opportunity one day to meet me and to let me know that she and my birth father were not trash." Countless birth parents tell about marking every birthday after making adoption plans for their children, of scanning the faces of youngsters at malls, movie theaters, fairgrounds.

Keeping the Right to Care

Wendy says she chose her particular home for unwed mothers because it was linked with an adoption agency that even in the early days of openness promised she could keep some degree of contact with Kristen's parents.

"I never forgot her and was determined to see her again," said Wendy.

While she was still at the home, Wendy even breastfed Kristen and held her up through a window so that Wendy's parents and Kristen's birth father, Donnie, could see her.

But even in that era, an unwed mother still meant an unfit mother. Wendy knew she needed to finish her nursing degree in order to support herself. Her social worker assured her she had helped Wendy choose adoptive parents that would give

Kristen a good education and Christian upbringing. In making an adoption plan for Kristen, Wendy knew she gave up her rights to rear her baby but not to care about her. When Kristen's mother sent the agency a baby photo to pass on to Wendy, "It really tugged at my heart," Wendy said.

Even Wendy's former boyfriend, Donnie, occasionally had thoughts about the daughter that he saw once even though he married someone else and lived for a while in a foreign country. "For twenty years I guess I lived in denial," Donnie said. "I thought I had just given her up, and that was it. But I was at a party and met someone who had made an adoption plan for her child. I confided that I had a child like that. The person I met said, 'I really believe you'll see her again.' I clung to that." Other birth parents who knew they had acted wisely in giving their child a better life still describe years of always carrying that child's image inside their heads.

> *I became more sensitive about the need to help birth mothers both before and after childbirth—for women who choose life for their children.*

After hearing so many agonizing tales like this, I was curious. Was that Eleanor's story? I wanted to know. Had she spent thirty years mourning and dealing with separation after birth?

Not really, she replied honestly. She claimed she trusted the doctor to choose well and that she had accepted the finality of it all. Although she cared deeply, she seemed to feel my existence less intensely—a situation I later learned was not uncommon to some birth mothers—and was able to put the unfortunate incident out of her mind, save for one report many years later. The wife of the doctor who made the adoption plan for me clipped out the newspaper story when I married. She sent it to Jean, the nurse, my birth mother's friend. Although Jean didn't pass on the clipping, she was able to communicate to my birth mother that I was doing well.

A Stunning Story

But the fact that Eleanor had basically put the birth from her mind was far less stunning than a story that would come later. It was clear to me that Eleanor liked us despite the fact we had known each other only a few weeks. She and Charles enjoyed being with us, found the whole concept of linking up with a grown child whom she hadn't had to discipline or support very satisfying, and thoroughly delighted in the little sprite who was Matthew.

Following an example set by Marty Renault, I began wearing a gold medallion that bore the inscription "I Found" and the historic date, May 10, that Eleanor and I talked for the first time. The medallion on a chain was a tremendous conversation starter and paved the way for me to share my story with anyone who would sit still long enough to listen. It seemed also to make Eleanor especially proud.

One night, however, she confided that no matter how happy she was to be located and no matter how thrilled she was with her new family in Texas, the truth was that if she had had the opportunity years before to end the life inside her, she would have. If abortion had been safely, readily, and legally available, she would have made it her choice when pregnant with me. It was the way she felt about things then—and it was the way she still felt about circumstances today.

Freelance writer Bob Rose said that his birth mother expressed the same emotion after he communicated with her the first time. "In our one brief meeting and two terse letters, she let me know that she wishes abortion would have been available in 1951. I have to endure the painful realization that

I am still not wanted by her. I also must live with the fact that I cause her pain, fear, and anxiety."[1]

Likewise, hearing Eleanor's story about wishing I could have been an abortion candidate is chilling. I'm thankful for the life I've lived, and to think I might not have had it at all is very staggering.

But in terms of affecting my self-esteem and making me feel, as Bob said, unwanted, truth was, very little ever did that—even learning that I could have been aborted had abortion been legal then. How could anyone reared with all the love that surrounded me fall prey to that kind of thought, albeit haunting?

The thought didn't affect my self-worth, but it did make me far more compassionate to the dreadful emotional pain that birth mothers face—the kind of emotional pain that would stay for a lifetime and that would prompt someone to wish a live, adult daughter with two precious children to be an abortion statistic.

I became more sensitive about the need to help birth mothers—to not only join in the cry to save the unborn but also to make life less traumatic—both before and after childbirth—for women who choose life for their children.

I will forever be grateful for Jean's parents who provided lodging for Eleanor during those months when she needed care far away from home. Once, after Eleanor told me the address of the modest, frame home where she stayed in Garland—only about a mile from where my parents lived at the time—I felt an overwhelming urge to visit there. I knocked on the door, told the current residents that my mother had lived there many years ago, and asked them if they would mind if I stepped inside briefly. I prayed that they would not fear granting entrance to a stranger, and I carried Matthew in my arms, thinking that a woman toting a pre-schooler would not look like a threat to anyone's security.

Once they invited me in (Louis watched from the car outside to be mindful of my safety), I strolled almost reverently from room to room, awestruck at the role that small bungalow had in ensuring my safe passage into the world. I could almost feel those plain walls still exude love and concern and support all these years later, and I paused a moment and said a silent prayer of gratitude for this. I departed as quickly as I arrived, but the few minutes I spent there were like a second homecoming—much like my visit to Colorado, because it was a return to a place I had lived before, after a fashion. I felt a great gratitude for the trend today of many churches to provide shepherding homes. Families volunteer to open their residences to single women who await babies. (In chap. 9 you'll read more about this practice.)

A Lifetime of Help

Unlike in my era, when agencies and physicians told birth mothers to "go home, start a new life, and forget this ever happened," birth mothers today are supported if they want to maintain contact with the agency. Counseling exists for birth mothers at any point in which they need help working through issues.

"My social worker [at the agency where she made the adoption plan for Kristen] told me I'd probably need some counseling after I visited with her for the first time," said Wendy, Kristen's birth mother. "She said, 'You'll feel really remorseful for all those years you missed.' I was glad she warned me, because I really had some sad moments."

Although their reunion was joyous, Wendy says she felt a great wave of sadness and ambivalence when Kristen's adoptive family showed some home movies of Kristen as a little girl. Other birth mothers report this intense sadness as they see photos of the adoptee growing up, since the photos are reminders of a life they might have had with the child but didn't and these are photos that they might have taken but couldn't.

"I watched them out of courtesy, but I had to swallow hard," said Wendy. Even though her reunion with Kristen and her family had been idyllic, Wendy was overwhelmed with the enormity of the what-might-have-been's and of all the years she missed. She said the event caused her to mourn for Kristen all over again, even though the two women by then had experienced a relationship for two years.

Kristen's adoptive parents saved the day because of their immense courtesy during this initial visit, Wendy said. "I was so nervous about meeting her family. I was afraid they would judge me. But they were just wonderful and so welcoming."

Wendy said she was grateful beyond belief that the agency was "there for me" and stuck by her during critical times while preparing her for this stressful yet rewarding moment in her life.

A Change in Responses

Ongoing care for birth mothers, with counseling provided throughout their lives like Wendy had, could have made a big difference in the response of their birth mothers, both Linda Sledge and Mary A. feel.

Linda's birth mother, who three years ago declined to meet Linda when the court-appointed social worker contacted her, told the social worker, "This [contact by a birth child] never was supposed to happen. This child never was supposed to have been able to find me."

"I can't imagine that she's never watched any of the [TV] talk shows," where the issue of finding a birth family is a frequent topic, Linda said.

Mary A. knows her birth mother received her registered letter introducing herself to her but has not responded. Mary says she has tried to make the letters sound as nonthreatening and newsy as possible. "I spent a lot of time in the letter focusing on her needs and how I had tried to understand what she went through, but she has not chosen to write back," Mary said.

Both Linda and Mary said they felt their birth mothers would have responded differently if they had been part of a post-adoption counseling program that helped them to see that such contacts were normal and to deal with issues unique to adoption.

Some of today's practices could have helped birth mothers of my era avoid agonizing all their lives over whether the child is all right. Despite the fact that her birth mother did not respond to her, Mary said she was gratified to learn from her searching that her birth mother was twenty-two when she was born. The fact that her birth mother gave birth to Mary when she was older consoled Mary that "I was a more minor bump in the road than if I had happened earlier." Mary, who received her doctorate several months after her first futile contact with her birth mother, said she had a great desire to let her mother know how life turned out for her.

Communicating that things turned out okay also has been a driving force behind nurse Tina Pewitt's endeavors to re-unite herself and two brothers, abandoned when they were preschoolers, with their birth mother. Tina said she wanted to meet her birth mother to bring peace to her heart about the years that had gone before. "I don't want her to have remorse. I would like to see her happy or to have the chance to make her happy. The fact that we are alive, some of us married with children, happy and well off—that is enough, surely, to please our birth mother."[2]

Roberta Williams sought to find the daughter for whom she made an adoption plan because she wanted to tell her she was loved. With the help of an organization that specializes in adoption searches, she found her daughter, who never had been curious because she had a happy, fulfilled life and was not aware of the emptiness that her birth mother felt. "It's the sweetest life has been for me," says Williams.[3]

God's Great Provision

More than any other realization, however, knowing my birth mother has made me more aware than ever of God's provision for me. This sentiment is echoed by Carolyn Wells as she recalls how God provided for her during those early years of abandonment by her mother.

Carolyn says that the mother who reared her "sent me to church to get rid of me" so she could be "unfaithful" without her adoptive father knowing. "Church became my family, and I began to see how Christian families loved each other. I felt that no one really wanted me, but I learned at church that God loved me." From an early age Carolyn believed that God intended for her to use her difficult family experiences to help strengthen families some day.

As a young adult, she married a minister, Ray Wells, and took some counseling courses while Ray was a seminary student. That propelled her to obtain her social work degree from Louisiana College, and today she directs the pregnancy/parenting/adoption program with Volunteers of America in Louisiana, where she counsels with many adoptive parents, birth parents, and adoptees.

"God has used all of those things to help me understand people," says Carolyn.

Likewise, Joe Wilson says meeting his birth parents "helped me put things in perspective. It killed any longing that I might have had about, 'Boy, I wish I'd grown up with them.' It makes me more content with where I am in life. I'm satisfied that my life is better. Even today, my birth mother doesn't regret her choices."

Betsy DeShano says learning about how her life was spared during her father's drunken rage that killed her mother "helped me realize how God was watching over me then and during my time in the foster homes until I could end up with parents who loved me."

It comes as no surprise that the "life passage" of Scripture for many adoptees—myself included—comes from Psalm 139—the beautiful verses that remind us what great extent God goes to keep up with the most minute of details in our lives.

> O LORD, thou hast searched me, and known me. Thou knowest my downsitting and mine uprising, thou understandest my thought afar off. Thou compassest my path and my lying down, and art acquainted with all my ways. For there is not a word in my tongue, but, lo, O LORD, thou knowest it altogether. (vv. 1–4)

Then this passage tells of some of the specific ways that God involves himself with us—ways that anyone, but especially adoptees, can relate to.

> Thou hast covered me in my mother's womb. I will praise thee; for I am fearfully and wonderfully made; marvelous are thy works; and that my soul knoweth right well. My substance was not hid from thee, when I was made in secret, and curiously wrought in the lowest parts of the earth. Thine eyes did see my substance . . . and in thy book all my members were written, which in continuance were fashioned, when as yet there was none of them. (vv. 13–16)

When I was being "made in secret"—before anyone, maybe even before Eleanor knew I was to be, I was no secret from God. He was there making plans for me and protecting me when I was being "curiously wrought." Weeks would pass before Eleanor would realize that an unplanned act had produced a child that she would spend the next nine months carrying and eventually separating from and the next thirty years wondering about. But God knew from that very first second, and He was in charge of things from the start.

God already knew that the product of that conception was Kay. Even though I sprang from an action of conception that wasn't meant to occur, and even when I was still a secret, God knew about the nurse's home in Garland and what a blessed way-station it would be. God knew about the doctor and his availability to help young women in difficult situations. God knew about Mable and J. D. Wheeler and the void that existed in their lives. God knew about Eleanor and her tiny embryo that someday would need a home. God knew she needed to have a plan that would work out best for both her and her child—a plan that would save her from social and financial ruin given the constraints of the era in which she lived and that would save her child from growing up amid shame and stigma. God knew about Eleanor's pain too, since He knew the pain of a birth parent in letting go of a child and gave His only Son in love to save the world, and He already was working to provide a means by which she eventually could resume her life in a healthy and whole way. God knew all this long before Eleanor even felt the first twinge of morning sickness and had to make a decision about being single and pregnant.

I was no secret from God. He was there making plans for me and protecting me when I was being "curiously wrought."

God "covered me in my mother's womb" even though that life may have seemed like a "mistake" at the time. On a broader scope, He covered all of us—all the parties in our particular adoption triangle—with love. And I am convinced that even then He was seeing a far more expanded picture than any of us ever could have visualized at that time. God could see the day that the child being made in secret would be a dandelion no more—the day that the gaps were closed and the questions were answered. I believe that, at least in my case, it was all part of His plan from the beginning. And as the psalm says, such knowledge almost is "too wonderful for me"! Thank You, thank You, Lord, for Your intricate care!

Using This Chapter

Adopted Persons

❧ Be prepared to hear birth parents' stories of pain and struggle—struggle that you may not have known was possible because of having grown up in happy situations. Many times adoptees are so caught up in the euphoria of a reunion that they aren't as sensitive as they might be to birth parents' tales of sorrow, shame, and abandonment. For many, the adoption represented multiple losses—loss of a child and loss of a relationship with their partner in the situation. Accept the fact that this may represent the first time the birth parent has felt free to talk about these feelings. Understand that the confession of these feelings is part of the healing in the birth parents' lives. Listen empathetically. Offer to pray with them. Thank God that they're willing to face the pain squarely in the face in order to provide you with the information you need.

❧ At the same time, don't feel responsible or let the pain of a birth parent's past affect your self-worth. The adoptee wasn't at fault because of the circumstances of the birth mother's life and wasn't to blame for the adoption practices of the day that kept healthy information from being exchanged. Don't feel that you have to make up to your birth parents in some way because of their heart-wrenching sadness. On the other hand, be aware of how much joy you can bring to these individuals' lives. It can't make up for their pain, but it can help give them peace and reassurance during the latter half of their lives.

❦ Expect facts first, then feelings, after a reunion occurs. Many birth mothers can more easily deal with factual matters about their lives, such as where they were born, where they went to school, and who their relatives are, than to tell how they felt about the incident that separated mother and child and about the feelings that engulfed them in the ensuing years. Be patient; usually the feelings will pour forth in time, but also be aware that repressing feelings has been how the birth parents coped over the years, since many virtually were told they had no right to grieve. Some birth mothers fear if they ever begin to let feelings out, a great dam will break and they won't be able to control themselves.

❦ Be aware that reunions can be brief and one-time or long and enduring. No two ways are alike, and no established pattern exists for an ongoing relationship between adopted person and birth family. Some people continue to see each other routinely and become an ongoing part of each others' lives; some relationships drop off after one or two contacts. Good, open communication is critical here. All sides can share about expectations and comfort level.

Adoptive Parents

❦ Continually emphasize with adopted children the aspects of how God brought you together as a family. The knowledge that God was overseeing the process will serve the adoptee well in later years when he or she learns about birth circumstances, especially if the child was born into an abusive home. Share with the adopted child how God revealed Himself to you in the midst of the adoption process. Continue to be mindful of how rearing a child amid love, acceptance, and affirmation is the best foundation possible if a child searches for birth family and learns of unpleasant circumstances.

❦ In a reunion situation, be sensitive to the feelings of birth parents when sharing details about the adopted child's growing up. Consider asking birth parents what's comfortable and what they most want to know about that time.

Birth Parents

❦ Be aware of counseling opportunities that exist today for birth parents. Contact the agency that helped you make your adoption plan, or look up one of the organizations listed in the appendix of this book to learn where you can join a support group or receive other help. The pain of separation from a child you give birth to is the pain of a lifetime; don't try to cope without professional help or group support.

❦ Help adoptive parents and adopted persons know your boundaries when they begin sharing about the child's life in the intervening years. If you feel overloaded with information or emotion, speak up. Most adoptive parents sincerely want to make this awkward time comfortable for everyone. They have as many fears and apprehensions and feelings of low worth as you do— and they will appreciate knowing what feels right and what doesn't.

SEVEN

The Relationships: No Carbon Copies

*M*y *relationship with my birth family* successfully leaped over the initial post-reunion hurdles (yes, we decided we would continue to write and call and visit; yes, we would become an ongoing part of each other's lives; yes, we would exchange Christmas gifts and birthday gifts and call each other up when red-letter days occurred in our families) and began to extend down into months and years. The period of astronomical phone bills and frequent airplane trips gave way to a more steady pace of regular contact; our dramatic year of firsts—first Christmas, first birthdays, first Mother's Day— observed together stretched out into a comfortable period that we saw would be permanent.

And yet there was still occasional high drama. One of those major red-letter days of our post-reunion relationship oc- curred when my half-sister Catharine married during the summer after we all met for the first time. Catharine asked Louis, who besides being a journalist was a licensed and ordained Baptist minister, to officiate at her wedding. I told her laughingly that I was thrilled that she conveniently waited to fall in love with Jeff until after we were part of the family and could participate in this event with her.

I felt especially cemented with her when Louis included in Catharine's ceremony parts of the vows and other key recitations that we had used at our own wedding eleven years before. When we wed, I had longed for my birth mother to know of this event and to be there to participate. Having Cathy and Jeff say "I do" to the same vows that were read on Louis's and my special day was one way of symbolically linking this family to another wedding many years earlier.

Louis's and my actual identities were known only to a handful of all the wedding guests—again, a matter that we left entirely to Eleanor's discretion. I could only shake hands with cousins and other peripheral relatives and friends and only survey them from a distance, but I did not feel deprived. I already had met personally most of those that I truly yearned to know. I was grateful to attend this large festive gathering— even anonymously—to help me gain a greater picture of my original family constellation.

A New/Old Family Name

Then the next summer, my sister Catharine acquired a name-sake when Catharine Louisa Moore arrived in our family— born on Eleanor's father's birthday. Although Catharine was the name we had picked out for a daughter years before, the name acquired heightened meaning after I met the Catharine who for years had been unknowingly significant in my life. We also learned that this name—with its uncommon spelling of two "a's"—appeared in many generations of Eleanor's family. Besides Cathy and Eleanor's great aunt, the name Catharine popped up in family genealogies for many generations. In fact, we pasted in Katie's baby book a photograph of her Aunt Catharine standing over the headstone of a long-ago Catharine from generations back. It was important to me that

Katie's name always would reflect the time in which she was born—when discovering my past and overlaying it onto the "me" I already knew would occupy such prominence in our lives.

It also thrilled me that Charles and Eleanor could share in and reap the rewards of the births of at least one of our children. Although they acquired Matthew as a three-year-old, they were part of Katie's arrival on the scene almost from conception. When I went into early labor and was bed-confined at six months into my pregnancy, Eleanor spent a week in our home helping care for Matthew and me as I rested. Eleanor and my mother and mother-in-law traded off weeks of bedside vigil, and this act made us seem knitted together all the more.

When I dressed a tiny seven-week-old Katie in a pink, ruffled frock, boarded an airplane, and took her to meet her birth grandmother for the first time, it was almost as stellar a moment as that unforgettable first time I landed in Colorado. And by then, my real identity was known to Eleanor's mother, and we were able to pose infant Katie with her birth great-grandmother in a four-generation photo that was very gratifying to me. Eleanor's mother passed away within the following year.

As Matthew and Katie grew, they came to delight in this extra set of grandparents. By the time Matthew and Katie were past babyhood, my parents were in their seventies and early eighties and seemed to genuinely rejoice in the fact that Matthew and Katie had a younger, more active set of grandparents, in their fifties and sixties, who could provide some lively experiences once my parents were past their prime. Having a zany and sometimes even boisterous Charles and Eleanor around gave an additional dimension to the lives of Matthew and Katie, and we—and my parents—felt God had provided this as a special gift to them. Following the splendid, open example my parents had set for me, Louis and I always explained to our own children with age-level appropriateness

Charles and Eleanor's unique role in our lives. Our kids grew up knowing and understanding the word *birth mother* in the same way I as a youngster comfortably had encorporated *adopted* into my vocabulary. Questions were answered frankly and fully. Sometimes at age eight and again at age twelve we'd go over the same territory explaining this unusual scenario once again, but we reviewed it and reviewed it until they understood.

More Fulfilling Information

When Louis and I moved to Plano, Texas, to be suburban newspaper editors and to live near my parents, seven years after I met my birth family—my mother stitched for me a wallhanging that contained quilt blocks Eleanor had given me on my first visit to Colorado. They were quilt blocks that her great-grandmother had pieced but never assembled, and they dated to the post-Civil War era. My mother, who is from a long line of seamstresses and needle artists, crafted the blocks into a stunning piece that had an even more stunning history. As I wrote in an article for *Quilter's Newsletter Magazine*, the quilt was more than just a work of needle-art. "It thrilled me to think of her stitches intersecting with those other minute rows that had been sewn long ago by another of my ancestors," I wrote about the "Reunion Quilt." To have this quilted treasure was rewarding, but to have the fulfilling family information that went along with it was something that grew more valuable to me with each passing year.

The genealogical information that accompanied knowing my birth family also held great fascination for me and provided a special source of enjoyment for Matthew and Katie as they grew. In tracing her family's roots back generations, Eleanor's line shared a common ancestor with Franklin D. Roosevelt. When our family toured FDR's Little White House in Warm Springs, Georgia, Matthew and Katie found the late president's family tree framed elaborately and hanging on the wall of one of the rooms. Instantly my children spotted the name of the ancestor I had told them about. From then on, FDR was the topic of many of their school research papers and term projects. It thrilled me that I, a person so rootless at one time, had provided this fascinating connection for my offspring. Marty Renault reported that pride in genealogical knowledge also represented a major reason why she was glad she had found her birth family. She said her husband Dennis "has done a lot of research into his Scandinavian roots, and I would have been so envious if I couldn't have traced my family line as well."

Another aspect that grew more cherished was the fact that I now had an avenue for knowing medical history.

Another aspect that grew more cherished was the fact that I now had an avenue for knowing medical history. Although Eleanor's family produced no blockbuster revelations of medical information, it was significant to learn that her mother had had a malignant breast tumor when she was in her eighties. Although not as critical to the breast cancer danger list as having a parent with a malignancy history, that bit of information put me into a slightly different category for mammogram frequency. And knowing of her family tendency to have arthritis has caused me to take preventive steps in that area as well. Having Eleanor's same general build and body structure, I felt it was prudent to be alert to the specific ways that she has been affected by that condition.

The thrill of learning physical resemblances never lost its novelty, even fifteen years after first verifying the mind-boggling family dental configuration. When Eleanor first saw the high-school graduation portrait of Matthew, who entered her life as a toddler but over the years grew to young adulthood, she was speechless. Finally, she managed the words, "My father. My father." In the portrait of her debonair grandson, all decked out in his tuxedo and bow tie for the graduation shot, she felt she was viewing her handsome dad as a young man. And as I heard those words, the former dandelion once again connected to a past generation.

A Share of Challenges

But for all the incredible coincidences, rewarding facts, and fulfilling connections, our reunion had its share of challenges—none so daunting they could not be managed, but challenges nevertheless. What began to emerge after some months was the fact that regardless of how many physical resemblances and bizarre coincidences an adoptee finds with his or her birth family, no carbon copies of oneself exists.

In meeting my birth family I felt I discovered a certain strain of my temperament that I couldn't track in my environs—a certain artistic bent that was helpful to identify. But that fact was far outweighed by the aspects of my personality that were totally dissimilar from theirs. Some of my personality traits I took the most pride in actually were traits that my birth mother found the most mystifying and the most difficult to relate to.

For example, I mentioned that I left no square inch of my house un-scrubbed and no recipe untried as I prepared for my birth mother's first trip to Texas to see my husband and son. I had an agenda for every minute of the weekend—a list of Houston sites I wanted them to see and people I wanted them to meet.

My meticulous level of organization was something I inherited from my adoptive family. It was a way that my adoptive mother and her sisters and mother communicated to guests that they were special and wanted. But this way of operating was foreign and even seemingly insulting to my birth mother and her husband. They had a fun-loving, anything-goes, spontaneous style. They were more comfortable leaving a schedule loose and filling in the gaps with the flow of things. During our first year of knowing each other, we purchased tickets for them to attend a Christmas drama on one of their visits to Houston. They declined to use them. We were puzzled since we had gone to such lengths to plan a special evening for them. They meant no offense, but they simply hadn't planned the trip to be scheduled so tightly.

Another challenging period occurred when my two mothers met for the first time. Remembering the photo of Marty Renault posed with her "two wonderful mothers," I always assumed I would be present when such a historic meeting occurred. I envisioned myself snapping pictures and standing by to soak up every word when these two key figures in my life first became acquainted.

In great detail I fantasized my mother's guiding Eleanor on a tour of her house and showing her quilts and her handwork and musing over the daughter they had in common. My dad, I imagined, would take Charles on a tour of his print shop and would point out in his back yard the two towering pecan trees that he had grown from twigs. My mother would serve homemade cookies and would be the quintessential, gracious hostess.

This poignant scene did happen, but it was not mine to witness. My parents and Charles and Eleanor did meet—on two different occasions, in fact—but not with me present at either event. This was Eleanor's preference—to take these steps privately, at her own pace, and in her own time. While my two sets of family spent two pleasant hours visiting, I spent two agonizing hours in my city five hours to the south, relying only on my imagination. I accepted Eleanor's wishes on this matter, but I certainly didn't like them. Only many years later during a third milestone visit would I even begin to understand and make peace with this development.

Negotiating Names

Determining what names to use was another concern. From the beginning we all were on a first-name basis. Calling

Charles and Eleanor anything that resembled mother or father didn't seem to fit, so that was never an issue. But for several years I felt awkward speaking of my adoptive parents as "Mother" and "Daddy" in Charles and Eleanor's presence. Even if we all knew our places in each other's lives, it seemed almost too cruel a reminder that those names belonged to someone else. A similar dilemma existed with our children. None of the nicknames that Charles and Eleanor proposed that Matthew and Katie call them seemed to roll easily off my children's tongues. Everyone thought it okay for the children to introduce Charles and Eleanor as their grandparents from Colorado. But after no nicknames took, our children soon lapsed into calling them by first names just as we did even though they said they felt disrespectful doing so. And even though the term now is in wide use, Eleanor never felt comfortable being introduced as my birth mother, so we lapsed into introducing them simply by name and hometown except to people who knew the story and who we could quietly pull aside before an introduction. It was a confusing set of dilemmas that I never would have anticipated encountering as part of a reunion. It reflected a whole new model for family that no etiquette book covered.

Then came the question of whether I would proceed to look up my birth father. By now my reunion with Eleanor and Charles had reached the point that I began to make inquiries about how I could find him. Doing so would not be difficult.

Eleanor had pointed out the neighborhood in her city in which he lived; she had seen him across the room in a restaurant once in recent years and was reasonably sure he was still alive. She had given me some basic facts about him such as hair and eye color, interests, and vocation. I had obtained from the city telephone book his address and phone number.

But as she provided those facts, she also stated a preference: "I'd really be more comfortable if you didn't look him up," she said. "It was a very painful time." This left me feeling puzzled and ambivalent. I likely would have respected my parents' feelings if they had felt strongly against my searching for my birth mother. Should I not do the same if my birth mother felt that strongly about my seeking paternal roots? I prayed that God would help me find the right answer for my life and the lives of all concerned.

What Other Adoptees Say

The challenges that I encountered in trying to forge a relationship with these closest of kin, yet strangers, are echoed by several other adoptees. "You know her, but you don't know her," Kristen Cunningham recalls thinking after her first meeting with her birth mother Wendy.

Some say the relationship is like adjusting to new in-laws with whom you are linked by marriage and yet are basically unfamiliar. But unlike in-laws, no one exists to "interpret" for you; a birth family comes without an instruction manual. After Louis and I married, I could explain to him that my mother's deep sighs were not a sign that she was offended or bored. They were merely her way of letting off steam as she coped with stress—the same way her own mother had let off steam. In meeting a birth family, finding this kind of an interpreter was equally, if not more, important than with an in-law family. Yet finding an objective person is often difficult—someone to help you decipher another's sighs, grunts, silences, rages, tears, or other patterns of behavior that are so critical to decode in a relationship.

Kristen's meeting her birth family took on an additional delicate twist—it paved the way for Wendy and Donnie, her birth parents, to reunite. Both divorced, the two began seeing each other again after Kristen contacted Donnie a year after she met her birth mother for the first time.

"It was like we had never been apart," said Wendy about her reunion with Donnie, whom she had dated for four years until Kristen was born. "Our personalities just meshed, just like they had then."

Kristen said she enjoys seeing the two of them together but says she would feel somewhat responsible if the relationship ended. "I just wouldn't want someone to get hurt," she said.

Tana Hill describes her relationship with her birth mother, who is nineteen years her senior, like this: "On some occasions, it could be close to mother-daughter; on some occasions, she's like another sister. We talk almost every day." But the relationship, though pleasant, has encountered some cultural differences. "I was reared in the city, and my birth mother and my sisters live in the country. I grew up in a church environment, and they haven't. It makes a difference in how we view things. I imagine there will be some subjects that we won't be able to talk about."

Jacqueline Jagger describes her nine-year relationship with her birth mother as "like a very good old friendship—there is an innate nature about it." But she says their communication is sporadic and relaxed rather than intense in nature—"a card in the mail from time to time, or she'll call."

Bill Wattendorf found that his birth father was an alcoholic—a situation which understandably limited the type of relationship they could develop. "For a forty-five-year-old man who was always drunk and a guy in his early twenties, we did pretty well," Wattendorf said. He said the relationship with his birth mother was comfortable because she did not have the parent-child history with him of being his disciplinarian. But Bill also felt he often had to play the adult to reassure his birth mother that he was not angry at her about the past.[1]

When social worker Carolyn Wells had her reunion with her birth mother, she found her to be a recovering alcoholic who had had "a lot of changes in her life" since the desperate days when she had to turn Carolyn over to an aunt to rear. "We visit about every three months and talk on the phone," she said. Carolyn said her mother at seventy-four is still in relatively good health. Carolyn believes they may have several good years left to make up for the years that they were estranged.

However, Carolyn said she has had to forgive her mother for leaving her in an adoptive situation that she says her mother knew was emotionally and physically threatening to her.

Joe Wilson said he found his birth mother, now happily married to a retired police officer, to be very nurturing to the children she reared, despite the fact that her first five children were removed from her because of neglect. "She would treat me like a son now if I allowed her to. To her it's like those thirty intervening years never existed," he said. But Joe says he has proceeded cautiously and has not thrown himself headlong into the relationship. "Even today, she doesn't regret her choices," he said.

Says Marty Renault about the difference in expectations and reality: "You fantasize all your life about these perfect people who are your birth parents. There's no way they could meet any of your fantasies." She says she advises adoptees to keep realistic expectations about the "very real people" they'll meet.

Overcompensating, Smothering

Sometimes adopted persons are caught off guard when birth parents want to overcompensate, either monetarily or in other ways, and make up for lost time. Sometimes birth parents, after their first painful loss, have been overprotective as they later built their own families. They may have been too intense with the children they did rear and find themselves "smothering" the adoptee—the only way they have ever known to relate to a child. If an adopted person as an adult has had a relatively independent relationship with adoptive parents and suddenly finds a birth parent freely giving advice or criticism, the results can cause some bumpy spots.

Betsy DeShano says early in her reunion she felt pulled and tugged by what she perceived were demands on her by both her adoptive and birth families. "In the beginning, everyone was threatened. My adoptive family was afraid my birth family would take me away; my birth family was afraid I wouldn't be around enough for them. I had to realize that I was only one person and that the road [to her families' houses] runs both ways."

Lorraine Dusky, who wrote the book *Birthmark* about finding the daughter for whom she made an adoption plan, says that birth mother and child are not mother and child in the traditional sense yet they are not friend and friend either:

> *Sometimes the adopted person will find someone with a highly different emotional framework.*

"These two people, connected in the most primal sense, are a little bit of both, straddling a gulf of time and circumstance, searching for a new ground." She writes that such a relationship, by its very nature, is bound to have its difficulties.[2]

Sometimes the adopted person will find someone with a highly different emotional framework with which the idealistic—and often very young—adoptee simply doesn't have the skills or frame of reference to cope. Sometimes adopted persons find birth parents who have long-buried family problems that led to their being put up for adoption in the first place.

The Right Timing

Although adopted persons can at any age reunite with their birth families, I was glad—and heartily recommend—that I waited to undertake my search until I was a "thirtysomething." By that point I had several major life events—college, career choice, marriage, and even three years of parenting—behind me. I was not attempting any other major life transition at the same time as I was forming a new identity that integrated biology and upbringing. Louis and I had been married for ten years and were seen in my adoptive parents' eyes as a separate family unit, thus making it less threatening for my parents; we were on our own anyway.

Jacqueline Jagger said she was glad she waited to find her birth mother until she had children of her own. "All during my growing-up years, I had told myself that she probably didn't care about me—or else why would she reject me? But after I had my first child, I knew so strongly that she must have loved me. It's just something that you can't know about until you're a mother. I understood then that for a woman to carry a child and nurture it with her own body for nine months and then be willing to allow someone else to love and raise that child was, what I feel, an unselfish and totally loving act." She said this realization that she was loved and that her mother had given up the dearest part of herself gave her great empathy for, and helped her be receptive to, her birth mother years later when Jacqueline had to do so for medical reasons.

Meeting my birth family after I was well into adulthood also lessened the strain for both my adoptive and birth mothers. My adoptive mother recalls hoping during my childhood that my birth family lived far away from Garland because she wanted to parent me with the freedom to make mistakes. "I didn't want to think that someone was looking over my shoulder passing judgment on my parenting," she recalls. Likewise birth parents attest to fears about adoptive parents' competence versus their own. The fact that my parents weren't in the middle of active parenting when I found Eleanor seemed to take the pressure off everyone and prevented the threat of competition on the parental competency score.

I also was glad that I had behind me the college experience of learning to live with many other individuals who were highly different from myself. My tolerance level—my ability to realize that many perfectly decent human beings existed that were highly unlike me and to accept as precious in God's sight even individuals with whom I did not mesh—had increased during my college years and young adulthood, as had my maturity as a Christian. Adopted persons who enter reunions with rigid expectations that they only will find carbon copies of themselves set themselves up for failure. The very forces—infertility, unplanned pregnancy, separation—that originally led to the adoptive situation inevitably produce a birth mother and birth child whose lives have been shaped by highly different circumstances and environments.

Linda Sledge says she was reared as "a highly cherished child as opposed to an unwanted 'extra' if I had stayed in my original family." That knowledge helps her understand why her mother hasn't consented to meet her.

Heather Guffee said the fact that she was seventeen when she searched for and found her birth mother may have been one of the reasons things "just didn't work out" after she looked up and visited with her birth mother six or seven times. "If I had waited until I was twenty-one, I'd have had the maturity to handle a lot of things differently than I did. It never occurred to me that somebody would be uncomfortable about having me in her life—which in itself is a tribute to how comfortable my [adoptive] parents have made me feel," she said.[3]

Who You Look Like in Spirit

As I processed my reunion experience during the fifteen years that intervened, two things that many other adoptees echo stand out.

First, while I was delighted to find people that I resembled on the outside almost as a mirror image, I was even more delighted to find those whom I looked like on the inside—in my emotional framework, in my spirit. These were my adoptive family, the people who changed my diapers, cried with me when I lost my boyfriend in the eighth grade, and stayed up all night putting hems in prom dresses. When all the layers were peeled away and all the facts were in, it was my environment that had shaped me. It was what I inherited psychologically that truly was at the core of my being.

It made me more grateful than ever to my adoptive parents. "I had no complaints about my rearing beforehand, but I had even fewer after I met them [my birth family]," said Tana Hill. "I love knowing them, but I wouldn't have been the same person if I had been reared there."

"I just needed that fulfillment. I've tried to turn it over to God."

Second, despite the trouble spots and the times personalities haven't meshed, most adopted persons who have the passion to search find the reunion experience altogether fulfilling and can't imagine what life would have been like had they not made contact. "It's a hard and scary step; it's not easy," said Tana Hill, who struggles with how she will blend long-term with the rural/urban differences that have surfaced between her and her birth family. "I knew I was opening a can of worms. But I just needed that fulfillment. I've tried to turn it over to God."

Marty Renault says the fact that she and her birth mother were separated for so many years makes them work extra hard at relating well and helps them be gracious about finding fault with each other. "I've bent over backwards not to have a fight," said Marty. "Because we're not around each other very often, we put up with a lot of idiosyncrasies when we're together. And there are just some subjects—like politics—that we don't talk about."

Lorraine Dusky wrote of her ten-year experience in knowing and forging a relationship with her daughter, "No matter how angry we've gotten, no matter how much trouble and turmoil, not knowing each other is unthinkable. I love her very much and cannot imagine my life without her in it.

Before, instead of the problems and pleasures that real people cause, we had only shadows to box with in our dreams. It was—there's no other way to say it—horrendous."[4]

Every year for the first ten years of our relationship, a white box bearing a dozen red roses arrived on Eleanor's door each Mother's Day. It bore a card which read, "For a mother who is very much alive." I wouldn't trade the whole world for that precious knowledge.

Using This Chapter

Adopted Persons

✣ Remember that no established pattern exists for post-reunion relationships with a birth family. Some find the ongoing relationship is smooth, some find it rocky, and some throw their hands in the air in frustration. It helps if individuals understand that reunions, even if much longed-for by all parties, reopen all the unhealed wounds that surrounded the initial events. The birth mother has carried the ungrieved loss with her for years in silence. Shame has been a part of the experience. In many cases the birth mother hasn't experienced the hope and healing and forgiveness that a relationship with God provides because she has felt condemned and judged. Birth parents have developed coping devices for those unhealed wounds, and agreeing to open them as part of a reunion experience requires tremendous courage. Sometimes all parties have to settle for less than they envision at the outset. Sometimes during the course of a reunion, a separation is important—detaching long enough to be able to view things objectively. Often the parties in the process come back more relaxed and more accepting of each other's differences.

✣ Don't expect that reuniting with your birth family will cause all your problems to be eliminated. While finding your birth family certainly goes a long way to bridge gaps and answer questions and solve great personal yearnings, it can never be a panacea for all of life's woes, most of which can have absolutely no relationship to your adoption. Expecting that a birth family meeting, though significant, will be a balm for all your ills puts too much strain on the reunion relationship and sets it up for disappointment.

Adoptive Parents

❧ Consider this an opportunity to minister to your adopted child. Help adopted persons accept disappointments or challenges that may occur in the relationship. Instead of feeling threatened or hurt, be a listening ear—the same way you would have been when your child sustained other confounding situations while growing up. Listen reflectively without giving advice. Even if you discouraged the reunion initially, avoid the I-told-you-so's if the situation has its rough moments. Stay supportive and helpful, and let the adoptee draw his or her own conclusions without your contributing judgment. Above all, pray for God's wisdom and guidance for your child in this critical juncture in his or her life.

Birth Parents

❧ Be prepared for how many areas of your life the reunion affects. It goes far beyond you and the birth child; it can alter your entire family dynamics. Your oldest child finds out another child is older than she is; the children that you reared may have to set aside the dream of being the ones to have the first grandchild. At least for a time, the adopted person becomes the center of attention, and children born into the birth family can feel displaced and may wonder what their position in the family will be now that the adopted person is on the scene. Be especially reassuring to your other children. Communicate that it is okay for them to ask questions and voice their fears and frustrations.

❧ Be aware that your thinking about yourself will change. You may suddenly find you are a grandparent and you may not be ready for the role. Take time for the adjustment, and be easy on yourself.

❧ Beware of wanting the adopted person to be like the children you reared, which he or she will not. Accept your birth child as an individual, and don't try to parent him or her as you would children that have been a part of your life for years.

The Support: Walking Through the Fire

✤

I was unprepared for the fact that I would spend many weeks and months after meeting my birth family actually in a daze. Marty Renault, the California artist whose finding her birth mother in LaMarque was so instrumental in my decision to search, told me this about her post-reunion experience: "It's like being in love the first time. You literally can think or talk about nothing else." Some adopted persons say people even tell them they look different—that their whole countenances are transformed—after this significant event in their lives.

The subject of my reunion managed to work its way into any conversation I had, no matter how unrelated. I'll never forget the day when I was interviewing four social workers for a newspaper article on the subject of job burnout. Somehow during the interview—on a topic completely unrelated to adoption—I lapsed into a discussion about my recent search experiences and completely forgot about my reason for the visit. "You'll have to pardon Kay; she's newly born," said the woman who arranged the interview, as she tactfully explained to the social workers the reason for my preoccupation. I was terribly embarrassed, especially since I normally was focused totally while on the job. I also usually was highly disciplined about not disclosing much personal information while I was working.

This situation was an example of how finding my birth family at first caused me to throw my old prudence out the window. It was as though laying a new "me" on top of the old one caused a temporary personality shift—one that I felt completely powerless to change. The social worker had spoken correctly. I *was* newly born in the sense that I now was viewing life as though through the fresh eyes of an infant, squinting in the bright light of truth that I knew and trying to focus on the world from that fresh, clean perspective.

During this crucial time—which lasted about a year for me but has been described as shorter or longer for others—the support of my husband, parents, and employer was absolutely vital. They buoyed me during a time when everything that I knew about myself was shifting. I am convinced that adoptees everywhere would still be trying to muster their courage to find their birth family and the progress that adoption itself has made during the past decade would still be set back years were it not for the role of this supporting cast—spouses, children, extended family, and friends who encourage and endure during the search, reunion, and relationship process.

Linda Sledge's husband Tim, a minister who has written several books on the subject of family dynamics, says that individuals who find their birth families become emotionally needy. They require much emotional support, in the same way a child going off to college, a spouse whose parent dies, or a child who transfers to a new school needs concentrated attention focused on him or her during those crucial times. "It's a time when your emotional underpinnings are all shaken," he said. "These are such big items of information that much of what you know about your world is altered. It changes your whole personal universe. It's almost too much to absorb. When we're adults, we normally don't add that much information to our personal data base, but adult adoptees are adding huge chunks to their personal data base." Tim was prepared for the fact that Linda would need much time and attention during the year of meeting her aunt and uncle from her birth family and being rejected by her birth mother and birth grandmother.

Despite the fact that her experience ended happily and didn't result in rejection by some family members, Kristen Cunningham also described herself as emotionally needy during that critical post-reunion phrase.

Said Kristen, "I would be in a daze for at least a week after visiting" her birth mother, Wendy. The same was true when she first met her birth father, Donnie. "You fantasize about what would have happened if . . .," Kristen said. The fact that her birth parents themselves reunited and began a new relationship only added to her absorption with the subject, she said.

During such times, Kristen's husband Grant was supportive and understanding and did not rush her through the processing. "It's difficult for anyone who is reared in their birth family to understand why you could become so preoccupied with this, but he was wonderful," she said.

Jacqueline Jagger said her husband comforted her while she was waiting to meet her birth mother by reminding her that the manner in which her birth mother would respond to the search was no reflection on Jacqueline's self-worth.

Jacqueline thought her husband was relieved to see what she might look like when she got older, since spouses sometimes can't help wondering whether some genetic skeleton lurks in the spouse's biological closet. "After he met Eva, he said, 'I hope you look just like her as you age.' It answered a lot of questions for him."

Another reason adult adopted persons need extra support is because of the "emotional ping-pong game that goes on inside them," said Tim Sledge. "You find yourself feeling all these dramatically opposite emotions. At one point in the meeting you're reminding yourself that 'I'm related to this person," and at another point you're asking yourself, 'I'm related, but can I really trust him?'"

Doing Some Legwork

Tim offered more than merely emotional support during Linda's search. Tim actually made some of the initial contacts for Linda with some family members. Where "Linda might have been too vulnerable" if a relative declined to reunite with her, Tim said he felt he could take a more detached approach to the process.

On some of these initial inquiries, Tim said he identified himself as "a minister working with a woman who may be related to you." He set up the first meeting between Linda and her birth aunt.

"That way, if the person said no, I would not feel the rejection she would," he said. When Linda started to experience "faintheartedness" in her search, Tim was there to press on. "When the situation would start to overwhelm her, and she would start to back off, I would continue to encourage," he said. "I wanted her to find out about her as much as she [wanted to]."

Tim made one dead-end trip to Oklahoma to gather facts for Linda and also went on a more productive fact-finding foray to look up state records in Austin.

Said Linda of Tim's role, "It's frustrating because you want to do [all the work] yourself, and yet I know I wouldn't have gone as far as I did in the search if he hadn't been there pushing behind me," she said.

Because of Tim's ministerial role as an intermediary, he had the opportunity to meet Linda's grandmother even though the elderly woman died before consenting to meet Linda. Although Tim said he regrets that he, and not Linda, had the chance to meet this family member, he feels that the visit still ultimately helped Linda.

"At least I was able to come back and describe her [her birth grandmother] to Linda," he said. "I was able to come back and tell Linda, 'This woman has your same type of skin.' It was a piece of the puzzle we hadn't had before then."

The involvement of Betsy DeShano's husband Phillip in her search and reunion with her birth family is especially poignant because Phillip was killed in a motorcycle accident several months after conducting a nationwide search to connect Betsy with her birth grandmother and two sisters.

"He had this desire to do something special for me," she said. Then, when Betsy met her birth sister and realized that the sister had recurring nightmares about her childhood in a troubled home, Phillip wanted to continue in the search until he got some answers that would help Betsy's sister. When Phillip died so soon after helping Betsy and her sister assimilate all this newfound information that would remove some of their fears and apprehensions about their birth family, Betsy said, "it was like it was time for him to go."

Less Than "There"

My family showed a tremendous amount of patience during some times when I was less than "there" for them in the immediate post-reunion time. Trips to the Texas State Fair with my family took on an entirely new perspective after I knew that Eleanor had attended this annual event in Dallas during her last months of pregnancy. During the first time our family visited the fair after I knew this information, I was more obsessed with picturing her as an expectant mother walking along the midway eating cotton candy than I was in watching my kids enjoy the amusement park rides. I was thankful that Louis had the objectivity to explain to my children why Mom seemed somewhat distracted.

I never could hear an ambulance screeching through the streets of Garland without thinking of her story about how Eleanor called an ambulance to take her to the hospital a week before her due date so that her delivery wouldn't occur on her birthday four days later. When such events like the screeching ambulance occurred, I literally drifted off as though to some other planet, and I simply was unreachable by my family for a while.

Daydreaming sometimes set in when I was at work. Sometimes deadlines for stories were missed because my energies were being channeled in another direction. My supervisor was tolerant; she, after all, had encouraged me in writing my adoption series for the newspaper and was more aware than the average employer would be about what prompted my distraction. I'll forever be grateful to my bosses for sticking by me until normal productivity returned.

Part of my catharsis during this period occurred when I wrote a poem, "Dandelion Song," (see pg. vii) about the impact of connecting with my native state of Colorado for the first time. The lines, "When you feel my step up on your soil, you may think it's a stranger's tread. But I'll learn to sleep beneath your stars with your valleys for my bed, for I'm your native daughter, though I had to be gone a while, but I vowed one day I'd find you if I had to walk every mile," reflected part of my emotional processing about having originated in that part of the country and incorporating those origins into my understanding of who I was. Charles Ward, the entertainment writer for the *Houston Chronicle*, set my original poem and tune to music, and I gave a copy of the musical score to my birth mother for a Christmas gift. Again, my family was understanding during the nights that I spent draped over the piano plunking out the melody for this song—totally oblivious to them while I was absorbed in this post-reunion project.

Remembering her own feelings of almost stupefied euphoria after she found her birth mother, Winnie, Marty Renault says she warns other adoptees in the early days of finding their birth family, "Be careful when you drive your car, and be careful when you figure your income tax. You're just not your normal efficient self."

Marty said she was grateful that she was not employed in an intensely demanding profession and that as an artist she could decrease her intensity until processing her birth information subsided. She said during that period, "I stopped painting landscapes and painted portraits of my family, since that's what I was thinking about anyway."

A Boost to a Marriage

Social worker Carolyn Wells said her husband Ray was "affirming and accepting" during the time several years ago when she "rebonded" with her birth mother, who was a family member and to whom Carolyn had related as an aunt during her growing-up years.

"Some of the stories that she told me were at first difficult to accept," said Carolyn. She said Ray's ability to love and accept people regardless of their background or unusual character traits helped her learn to forgive her birth family members for some painful incidents of her childhood.

"In our early marriage, I had a struggle for intimacy because of some of my childhood experiences," she said. "I hadn't realized how they had affected me and how they would affect a marriage relationship."

Carolyn said she and Ray together read many self-help books that showed them what issues from her childhood need to be worked through. She said Ray himself benefited from this introspection to give him a heightened and improved understanding of his own childhood.

Spouses who support an adopted person through a search and reunion aftermath are willing to make the investment because they see how it benefits the marriage in the long-run—even though they may perhaps bear the biggest part of the psychological aftermath. Some spouses help because they realize that it's difficult to give yourself totally to another person when you may not even know much about your real self—unless you search for your birth family.

When Louis and I married twenty-five years ago, we pledged in our wedding vows to each other's "self-fulfillment as a person." Little did he realize how that pledge would be tested during the time I sought to close this hole in my heart by tracking down and meeting my birth family. From a practical standpoint, it benefited us as a couple because we now had more complete medical information to use as necessary for ourselves and our children. The realm of secrecy was removed and the blank spaces filled. We could deal much more easily with the facts than with suppositions.

> *We now had more complete medical information to use as necessary for ourselves and our children.*

"Anytime you know more about who you are, that helps a relationship," said Tim Sledge about why he believes that helping a spouse search for his or her birth family helps a marriage. "There's an inner peace that comes out of knowing who you are. Not knowing added to the stress that Linda was under. It's also a shared experience. It's one of the big things I've been able to do for her."

Assets in Objectivity

Spouses also are great assets in objectivity. My husband was invaluable in helping me see myself objectively in light of all the new information I was receiving. For him it was akin to standing on the boundary between two states and being able to survey both areas from his unique vantage point. From his unique vantage point in my life—knowing me intimately as a spouse does—he could assess how both heredity and environment had contributed to shaping me as a person. Unbiasedly, he could spot mannerisms, personality traits, and physical connections that were beyond my ability to recognize. He could provide a perspective that few others could because he knew all parties and could analyze the situation in a helpful and accurate manner. It thrilled me when he told me that he thought that I had "inherited" my adoptive mother's warm, open, affirming personality and industrious nature—something only he could identify.

In those early days when some of the family members I met were reluctant to express feelings, Louis often helped me look beyond words and see actions that were signs of love when flowery phrases were minimal. Spouses also can help adoptees keep good psychological boundaries and be on guard if the relationship looks as if it may be taking some dangerous emotional turn. He also helped remind me to keep proper contact with my adoptive parents—to be at all times verbally reassuring and to keep them posted on all new developments. Without his guidance, it would have been so easy—and so destructive—to neglect that relationship while I was preoccupied with the other, new one.

> *Spouses can help adoptees keep psychological boundaries and be on guard if the relationship looks as if it may be taking some dangerous emotional turn.*

Tim Sledge's understanding of family-of-origin issues helped Linda process the rejection by her birth mother and birth grandmother. "I was able to help her understand the tragic effects that what therapists call 'the rule of silence' has on families," he said. "After Linda's mother gave birth to Linda, the matter was never discussed in her family. Even Linda's mother's aunt wasn't told. They told her that Linda's mother went away because she had a nervous breakdown. It was something that just didn't happen. It's no wonder, then, that when Linda surfaced later, the attitude was, 'This person isn't supposed to exist.' They had tried to deny her existence all these years."

New Sets of In-Laws

Spouses also are affected because they acquire an entire new set of in-laws when a husband or wife finds the birth family. In our case Louis had hammered out a successful relationship with my parents during the ten years we had been married, only to be faced with starting again with a new set. Again, the lack of an "interpreter" surfaces since both spouses—not just one—may not have a clue what certain gestures, phrases, and behaviors mean in the context of the family. A husband can't pull his wife aside and say, for example, "Now, when your birth mother walks through the house slamming doors, does that usually mean that she's angry about something?" because unlike in a regular in-law situation, the spouse who is the birth child does not understand these new family members' style or jargon or body language.

Paul's words to the Ephesians about husbands and wives represent exactly what is demanded of the marriage in which an adoptee-birth family search or reunion has occurred.

Carolyn Wells said that husband Ray was good-natured about acquiring not only two but three sets of in-laws as a result of her birth family situation. Carolyn said she entered the marriage knowing her birth father and his wife, birth mother and her husband, and the parents who reared her. "There never were any secrets about my complicated family, and he was willing to take me on anyway," she said.

Some delicate post-reunion situations can set in when spouses feel left out of the process. Tim Sledge says he and Linda have discussed his concerns that "she'll get close to her new family and I won't. I see them all start to connect, and sometimes I feel like the outsider. They're really all into this, and I feel sometimes peripheral." Tim says he feels especially vulnerable on this topic since he did not have a close relationship with some of his own family members.

Although this is a potentially painful aspect of Linda's post reunion, Tim says he feels he and Linda are fortunate to have good communication patterns so they can openly discuss his reservations. "It would be especially crucial for spouses to have good communication before they put this kind of stress on their marriage," he says.

Mutual Love

As supportive spouses walk through the fire with husbands or wives involved in some aspect of adoption, they are embodying the apostle Paul's admonition to spouses about mutual love and support (see Eph. 5:22–25). Although at the time he couldn't have known about the contemporary dilemma of finding a birth family, Paul's words to the Ephesians about how husbands and wives should have mutual respect and love for each other represent exactly what is demanded of the marriage in which an adoptee-birth family search or reunion has occurred.

A Door Left Closed

Despite all they had been through to support me in this reunion, my family urged me to contact my birth father. But after considering it off and on over a period of several years—and making it a matter of much prayer—I decided it was a door I would not choose to open. For several years after meeting Eleanor I had gathered some basic facts on how I could contact him. Looking him up would be simple enough, since I knew—and had even driven around in—his neighborhood, also in Colorado. I had seen his photo, and certainly I was curious to know more. To decline to make this contact would still leave me with only a partial picture of myself, and certainly his side of the story—and his medical information—was important, too.

But just as every adopted person must decide whether searching for his or her birth family is the right step for him or her, every person who searches has to decide at what level a saturation point is reached. In my case, I had achieved a comfort level that was workable, and I felt at peace about what I knew. I felt that the connection I had established with my birth family through my birth mother was the main one I was seeking. Unless in the future I strongly felt God's leadership to the contrary, the gaps that existed from the paternal side of my family tree would have to remain gaps. I felt that I had enough information about my birth father to suffice, but I also know that even that information might not be satisfactory for my children someday. I did not rule out the possibility that in their adulthood, they might choose to open the door that I had elected not to look behind.

Adoptee Tana Hill echoed the same sentiments after she met her birth mother and numerous members of this family. Tana learned about several abilities and physical features she inherited from her birth father's family and met some paternal relatives. She learned, however, that her birth father, who is married and has three children, "is not willing to accept" a reunion. Tana said about the prospects of meeting him: "It's not a must for me."

Some adopted persons seek the help of a family therapist or other mental health professional to adjust to what they've learned about their past. Betsy DeShano said she needed a therapist's help to process some of her guilt feelings after she learned about the circumstances of her birth family and her father's murder of her mother. In talking to relatives, Betsy learned that she was a colicky infant. She began to fear that her colic could have pushed her already-stressed father over the brink and caused him to take her mother's life.

"I felt as if it was my fault. My counselor helped me realize that I was an infant and that I had nothing to do with it. It was my father's problem in how he reacted to life's circumstances," she said.

How Churches Can Help

Churches also can help in walking through the fire with parties in the adoption triad. I'm thankful for the many people at my church who knew I was in the process of searching and who offered to pray for me at critical junctures in the experience. Suzanne Arguello writes about what churches can do to minister to persons in the adoption process, and her words can apply just as easily to adopted persons who are searching and adoptive parents who are struggling to know how to support and encourage their children. She wrote about an adoptive couple, Janice and Jim, who routinely make personal contact with couples in the church who were involved in adoption. She wrote that Janice's personal collection of books on adoption became a lending library for couples at various points in the adoption process. Janice also purchased extra copies of the most popular books and donated them to the church library.

> *Churches should avoid treating the subject of searching as though it is some deep, dark secret.*

"Janice spends hours on the phone encouraging women about adoption, praying with them, counseling, crying, and comforting them with verses of Scripture. They [Janice and Jim] have even started an informal support group for couples and families" she observed. [1]

Churches can link up people who have been through this process. In our own church are literally dozens of families who have been affected by adoption in some way, including several adult adoptees who have found their birth families. Churches should avoid treating the subject of searching as though it is some deep, dark secret. Pastors, church leaders, and fellow members can ask the adopted person questions such as, "How is your search going?" or "How are things with your birth mother?" This topic is usually high in importance in the adopted individual's mind. Having another resource as a sounding board may relieve pressure from the marriage, also, because it provides someone else with whom the individual can reflect and let off steam.

Numerous church friends have invited me into their homes to talk to their young son or daughter who is an adopted person. They have encouraged their children—usually elementary-school aged or an occasional teenager—to question me about how I felt growing up adopted and what it was like for me to be curious about my birth family. This is a ministry that many adult adoptees would be happy to perform if asked.

When churches have birth parents in their fellowship, they can help these persons through their grieving and loss and not feel outcast.

Many adopted persons and adopted parents have processed the adoption-related events in their lives as part of their Christian pilgrimage and would be delighted to speak to groups in their church about their experiences and how the Lord has been real to them in the process. I'll always be grateful for the time the chairman of our church's deacons asked me to talk about my adoption and reunion experiences as I gave the devotion before the deacon body. Many in the audience had never thought about how such an event in a person's life could be used for God's glory, and I was thrilled to be able to share what I had experienced.

Youth groups can schedule panels of people who are involved in various aspects of adoption—adult adopted persons, adolescent adoptees, adoptive parents at different stages, and even birth parents who have made adoption plans.

(In chap. 10 I will share what occurred when I participated in such a panel with our church's youth group.) Such a panel gives youth who are adopted an opportunity to hear others like them and exposes them to some of the ethical choices they may make.

When churches have birth parents in their fellowship, they can help these persons through their grieving and loss and not feel outcast. Churches can sponsor support groups for these individuals. Christ-centered support groups on self-esteem and processing painful pasts can help these individuals experience hope and healing as they learn about the unconditional love of God.

Likewise, birth mothers need lots of support as a search or reunion hits them afresh with the undeniable reality of an act that happened years ago. Reunions might not ever occur were it not for spouses like Charles who encourage the meeting and visits afterwards and who do not feel threatened because of the specter of an earlier relationship that the adoptee no doubt brings to the scene. If birth mothers should surface in a church setting as more and more adopted persons link up with their heredity, churches can recognize that these are people in need, just as a church can support anyone going through a crisis, such as a job loss. Churches can celebrate this event with individuals without judging or blaming—and without making this incident a matter of gossip.

Oklahoma church worker JoAnn M., whose daughter made an adoption plan for an infant three years ago and who asked that her last name not be used, said churches also need to be sensitive to the needs of birth grandparents.

"We didn't sense that any of our friends pulled away," she said. "It was very important to us that our friends just went right on and treated us normally. They don't hold back in their discussions about their grandchildren when they're around us, even though they know that our grandchild is not with us."

JoAnn said that she appreciated the support of her church staff members when she and her husband received a critical anonymous letter during their daughter's pregnancy. The minister urged them to discard and not read anything that was unsigned and with no return address.

However, J. J. Cunningham, a retired pastor, said he was stunned by the mood of silence that prevailed when members of his congregation learned that his grandson had become a single parent and had made an adoption plan for the child that was born. Cunningham said the devastation he and his wife felt about this incident was obvious to fellow church members—especially when he wrote about it in a magazine that circulated in his denomination—but the kind of emotional support he needed from others in the congregation was less than he expected.

They need to see the heart of the church during this time.

Cunningham said grandparents have the same feelings of inadequacy and guilt and experience the same "what if's" as parents do in these situations. Although Cunningham knows that adoptees now have more freedom to find relatives in later life, he worries that he might not be alive when this occurs. "It makes me wonder how old I'll be before I'll be able to tell this little girl that she has a great-granddaddy that loves her," he said. He said he was thankful to be able to confide in a pastor friend in a neighboring town when he needed support.

JoAnn said she was grateful that her church continued to allow her daughter to have leadership roles in the youth group during the early part of her pregnancy. She said an older youth offered to drive her places she needed to go. As a result of the way her church reached out to her daughter, JoAnn has become involved in working with pregnant teenagers.

"You can offer to take them out for a soft drink, to drive them places, to let them live in a spare room," she said. "Some people say if we make it easy on them, they will keep getting pregnant. But the girls aren't thinking about that; they're thinking about survival. They're thinking about just getting through the next day. They need to see the heart of the church during this time."

Using This Chapter

Adopted Persons

❦ Have a support system in place as you enact a search and reunion. A supportive spouse or other family member is ideal, but if this isn't possible, make certain you know people at your church, in your neighborhood, or among your friends who can hear your heart on this issue. Call them when you need a boost or an encouraging word.

❦ If your spouse doesn't tune in to your needs, encourage him or her to talk with other spouses who have been a part of a search and reunion. The person perhaps can help your spouse see the benefits to the marriage and understand your pilgrimage.

❦ Locate a professional Christian counselor with whom you can reflect about your feelings. Finding and reuniting with your birth family is far too major a life issue to go through without professional support.

❦ Be aware of information overload. You may arrive at a point in which your mind has absorbed its limit of new and life-altering information. Don't hesitate to slow down and let yourself process before you gather more.

❦ Be aware of the disorientation and preoccupation that occurs when you find your birth family. If you possibly can, avoid scheduling a reunion period during a time in your life when other major events, such as marriage, childbirth, or job transition, occur.

❦ Find outlets such as writing, painting, sculpting, or whatever creative means you use to vent feelings. These can be critical to your equilibrium during this high-stress time.

❧ Be respectful of other family members who may need you to be available to them. Perhaps you can schedule your times to process and debrief during hours after children are asleep and after work deadlines are met.

Adoptive Parents

❧ Keep good lines of communication open with your adopted child. Try to be understanding and patient as the adopted person adjusts to this realignment of his or her life, but don't hesitate to speak up if you feel left out or if you need more input. Don't expect your adopted person to initiate all the contact; do your share.

❧ Help educate your church about awareness of adoption-related issues. Offer to speak about your connection with adoption.

Birth Parents

❧ Follow much of the same advice to adopted persons. Find a support system, locate a professional Christian counselor, find creative outlets, and try to pace yourself without taking on additional stress if you're in the middle of a search and/or reunion process. Speak up for your needs during this time.

❧ Seek the counsel of a therapist to help your spouse and children deal with new information about your past that may surface during this time. Remember that through Jesus Christ, God has provided a means by which our self-worth is not based on anything that has occurred in our past but on God's forgiveness and His unconditional love.

❦ Understand the passion and preoccupation with which the adopted person enters into this time (or if you're the party searching, the passion and preoccupation may be yours). Try to keep your life simple while you are adjusting to the new events in your life.

The Climate Today: A Better Mousetrap

✿

*I*t was a Saturday afternoon—a time that usually finds
families enveloped in errands or carpooling to softball practices or enjoying some leisure activity to rest from the weekday
rat-race. But people in the audience that packed the meeting
room and fringed its aisles, waiting patiently to hear a speaker
whose plane was more than an hour late, seemed perfectly
content to spend their weekend afternoon just where they
were.

I had traveled by special invitation from my home in
Nashville, where our family several years earlier had moved
from Texas to live, to address this Houston meeting of adoptive parents, adult adopted persons, birth parents, and others
affected by adoption. Other than shifts in hairstyles and
fashion, they differed little from the Houston audiences that
I addressed routinely more than a decade ago after my public
story about finding my birth family thrust me actively onto
the nationwide speaking circuit about adoption matters. The
passion for the topic that kept them glued attentively to a

speaker in the midst of a busy weekend was no less intense than it was ten or fifteen years ago when topics pertaining to the adoption triad were raised. They plied their questions with the same mixture of zeal and anxiety and concern that people involved in adoption did when the adoption reform movement first gathered steam in the late 1970s. And their questions followed the same lines as they had back in those early days:

⚜ Should I search?

⚜ How will I answer my children when they start to get curious?

⚜ How much should I tell them?

⚜ What will my adoptive parents think if I find my birth family?

⚜ What do I do if my birth child searches and reenters my life?

⚜ How can I be sure I won't lose my adopted child's love if another set of parents enter the picture?

But one marked change had occurred that made it much easier and more rewarding to address such a group of adoption-related persons. In those intervening years, adoption had built a better mousetrap, and that fact made it easier for a speaker like me to offer hope.

A Different Reaction

This better state of adoption perhaps was best illustrated by a comment that an adoptive father voiced at the end of my talk to the Houston audience that day. "We've already decided that when Margie wants to look for her birth parents, we'll help her," he said. I compared this reaction, which now is more commonplace than controversial, with one I heard bellowing at the other end of the telephone line in July 1979, the day after my adoption series ran in the *Houston Chronicle*. At that time an adoptive father scolded me with these words: "People will stop wanting to adopt if they think their children will grow up to be as ungrateful as you."

In the late 1970s, when radical social change in adoption practices was about to sweep the country, maverick adoption agencies began to take a more enlightened approach to the psychological severing that occurs when birth parent and adopted person are separated. Alert to the impending shifts in the way people soon would practice adoption, some astute agencies began to suggest to their birth mothers to contact the agencies and update their addresses so that matches could be made when and if state laws sealing adoption records changed.

In the wake of those early ground-swells, some agencies began facilitating the exchange of letters between birth parents, adopted persons, and adoptive parents. The letters provided no identifying information but allowed the parties in the adoption process to correspond with each other, with the agency acting as the intermediary to pass on the letters. The impact of this letter exchange on the people involved "was obvious and immediate," wrote Kathleen Silber and Phylis Speedlin in their book, *Dear Birthmother*, which published a collection of some of these tender, yet on-target letters. Silber, then director of Lutheran Social Services Agency in San Antonio, wrote that she, as a professional in the field for years, had followed the traditional adoption philosophy which demanded that a birth mother be cut off from her child as much as possible and that adoptive parents know as little as possible about the genetic roots of the child they reared.

However, when the first letter exchanges occurred, Silber was struck by "how healthy it all seemed—how relieved everyone was." Adoptive parents were relieved to hear the birth mother's assurances that she cared for her child but never would do anything to intrude on the adoption, and birth mothers were relieved to hear that their children were well-loved, happy, and healthy. Moreover, the letters provided a means to help the child eventually know that the birth mother indeed had loved him or her very much.[1] Such exchanges paved the way for the more open approach that soon would follow.

A New Wave of Openness

Today, a growing number of adoptive parents are like Beth and Brian Fellers, who met their daughter Brooke's birth mother during her pregnancy so that they could establish a relationship before the birth. The birth mother chose them from an album of profiles of potential parents the agency provided her, and couple and birth mother began to socialize so they could get to know each other in a relaxed setting. Brian, a minister of music at a church, laughs a little as he looks back on one of those first meetings. "We fumbled around a good bit," he says about his and Beth's first attempts at conversation with Brooke's birth mother. "We wanted to make a good impression. When we found out she had chosen us, we asked her if we could send her roses. Later we found out that she made us an album starting from the time when she got the roses."

"If they can spend some time together before the baby is involved, they can get to know each other as people."

After Brooke was born and her birth mother returned to her home, the Fellers have sent pictures and letters as the baby has grown, and the birth mother has visited Brooke twice—once on Brooke's birthday and once at Christmas.

"If they can spend some time together before the baby is involved, they can get to know each other as people," said Carla Monroe, director of Baptist Children's Homes Maternity and Adoption Services in Illinois, in describing the kind of open adoption that the Fellers and many others have participated in. "We even ask couples if they would like to be at the hospital when the birth occurs. The couple gets to begin bonding with the baby as soon as an hour after birth. For the birth mother it's reassuring to see that they really love the child, and adoptive parents don't have to wonder what kind of person the birth mother is. To date, all adoptive parents have viewed it as a positive experience. It's as close to a pregnancy and birth as you can get without actually giving birth to the baby."

> *"It's as close to a pregnancy and birth as you can get without actually giving birth to the baby."*

Other couples choose varying degrees of the openness the Fellers experienced. Vast numbers of agencies for many years have allowed the birth mother a say in the placement—even to the point of allowing her to choose her child's adoptive family from among candidate profiles. But now the way agencies practice adoption has changed so drastically that adoptions that have been tagged "customized" or "designer" exist today, with individuals choosing what form matches their comfort level. "It's pretty much whatever the parties work out," says Sylvia Franzmeier, senior director of postadoption services for Houston's DePelchin Children's Center, one of the early forerunners in the trend toward openness. Some adoptive families and birth parents may prefer merely to have the agency forward letters and photos with no contact; others may prefer to have a one-time meeting at the time of placement without revealing last names.

Some, like Christian writer Ann Kiemel Anderson, who has adopted four sons and has known each birth mother in advance, have been present in the delivery room at the time of birth,[2] beginning a relationship that can continue throughout the child's life if everyone is willing. At whatever point in

Agencies' post-adoptive services programs are making a major difference in the way all parties of the adoption triad live out their situations.

the process meetings occur, caseworkers usually are present to help break the ice and to make sure that despite the emotion and high drama of the moment, helpful information is exchanged.

"We decided secrecy in adoption is harmful," said Dr. Aileen Edgington, executive director of Hope Cottage maternity home and adoption agency in Dallas. "The child goes through life wondering, 'Who am I? What are my roots?' With an open adoption, answers are out in the open."[3]

Even some of those who originally protested have changed to meet the needs of the times. In 1992, Gladney Center in Fort Worth, one of the nation's oldest and largest adoption centers and maternity homes, reversed its 104-year-old policy of maintaining an absolute barrier of secrecy and began open adoption. As part of its ongoing counseling program, Gladney arranges contacts between adoptive and birth parents, but if those involved want to exchange addresses and meet on their own, the agency steps aside. Now 20 percent of Gladney's adoptions involve some degree of openness, and the agency tells parents that being willing to establish contact with the birth mother may help them adopt sooner.[4]

"They really stretched us in terms of what we'd be able to accept," said Brian Fellers about the period when his agency first proposed open adoption. "It was really scary at first, but they don't make you do anything you aren't comfortable with. The idea grew on us."

Other Helps

But these customized adoptions, though dramatic, are not the only methods during the past two decades that have made adoption a more healthy practice. Agencies' post-adoptive services programs are making a major difference in the way all parties of the adoption triad live out their situations.

Agencies now provide a myriad of services for families to help ensure that the adoption is successful. Adopted persons can return to the agency with their questions and for guidance about how to go about searches and reunions; adoptive par-

"We tell the birth parents that we're here as long as they need us."

ents can learn how to deal with their child's curiosity, and birth parents can return any time to grieve and seek counsel.

"We are aware that there are many times that emotionally impact these young women, such as the first-year anniversary of the child's birth or when the birth mother gives birth to her first child that she will rear," said Carla Monroe of Baptist Children's Home. Holidays like Mother's Day also can be traumatic for them, as these women find themselves wondering, "Was I really a mother? Did I really give birth?" Monroe says her agency counsels them and tries to get them into support groups with others. Some support groups across the country for birth mothers help them determine whether searching for their birth child is a possibility; others merely offer an avenue for birth mothers to express their emotional pain in the company of birth mothers. Sandy Ivey, director of a branch office for Bethany Christian Services, says, "We tell the birth parents that we're here as long as they need us."

"It is the courage of these [birth mothers] to come back to these agencies and talk about their experiences that has made agencies more compassionate," says Carol Demuth, head of Hope Cottage's education and support services. "We are in the midst of change, but we still need to be a lot more humane in the way we think about birth families."[5] Counseling also is available for birth grandparents, who may be grieving for the loss of their birth grandchild or about the fact that their daughter or son didn't fulfill their heart's desires.

Ongoing Support to Birth Families

Part of the work agencies do with birth parents is to encourage them to be totally honest with their immediate family—when it looks as if the birth parents are about to marry or after the children that they rear are old enough to understand. "We tell them when they're pregnant and still with us that this event is very critical to who they are," Monroe said. "It's not something they'll ever forget. We strongly encourage them that when their children are old enough, to tell them, 'I had a child earlier in my life before I met your father (or mother),' so that it's not a major shock when that adopted person appears conducting a search."

In a tribute to the birth mothers in its history and in an effort to communicate ongoing support to birth families, Hope Cottage in Dallas held a historic open house for families who made adoption plans for their children, and three other Dallas agencies hosted similar open houses on the same day.[6] Hope Cottage even sponsored a picnic at which some birth parents who have maintained contact with their birth children and their children's adoptive parents attended.[7]

Acknowledging that the teen years can be a tough time for adopted teens and parents, many agencies have post-adoptive support programs that help parents with special issues that crop up in adolescence. Some even have support groups for teen as well as elementary-age adopted persons. As part of its post-adoption services Bethany's monthly newsletter contains a column about special issues that arise in parenting adopted children. In one newsletter, the column focused on helping parents of teen adoptees understand what they can do to make things better for adopted teenagers. It advised parents to provide a sense of connectedness by letting teens know that parents are there for them, to embrace the differences their child brings into the family to acknowledge that although differences exist between all family members, each is a valuable member, and to be an advocate for their teen by seeking the birth history and background information of the child. The column said that adopted teens often feel that they have no control over past events in their lives, and this may result in increased sensitivity to the issue of control—which may result in defying authority figures. Parents were advised that teens "may have some additional adoption baggage, but with understanding and commitment you and your child can stand firm together during the turbulence of this journey." [8]

Being with Others Like Them

Annual adoptive parents picnics which agencies frequently sponsor as part of ongoing care to families are valuable because "they allow adopted children to be with others like them—to help them realize that they belong to this great body of people," said Bethany's Sandy Ivey. For example, at such events, "the adoptive parents with a ten-year-old can counsel adoptive parents of a six-year-old" about what to expect at that stage, she said. "The support they provide for each other is far more than anything we can provide them."

Even for those who don't want open adoption (Ivey, for example, says only about one third of all the adoptive families in Bethany's Tennessee caseload want face-to-face meetings; at DePelchin Children's Center during 1993 about half met face to face with the birth family) agencies provide plenty of assistance to help parents with questions that arise. When Margaret Mary Hays at age eight had questions about her birth mother, her parents Jud and Cookie handed their daughter a computer printout their agency provided. The printout contained birth family information like color of hair and eyes, age, nationality, and some interests. The fact that the Hays have an official agency document containing information helps Margaret Mary feel she knows everything the parents know, said Cookie.

Although her daughter Jenna was adopted before the days of open adoption, Paula Arrington says she appreciates the help their agency rendered when Jenna, as a junior high student, returned to the agency to talk with the social workers. Blake, their son born to them after Jenna was adopted, went, too. Jenna said of the session, "I found out that I was American Indian, that my birth mother likes to read and is mild-tempered. I know that she had straight blond-brown hair. They told me that they'd contact me if she ever contacted them." Jenna said this met her need at that stage in her life.

Bracey and Gay Campbell learned from their agency that their daughter Jenna's birth mother had athletic ability and excelled in gymnastics; as a result they made those kinds of classes available to Jenna, eight, when they might not have known to offer her training in this area otherwise. Already they can see her natural skills unfold and aptitudes in this area emerge. "She's in her fourth year of gymnastics, and she can climb a rope twenty feet up in a heartbeat," said Bracey. The agency also told the Campbells that Jenna had a birth parent who was an accountant, which they feel may explain Jenna's adeptness at math. The helps their agency has provided both before and after adoption have made them pleased with their decision. "I just can't express to you the joy I've found in adoption," Bracey said. Gay says there's "not one bit" of difference in the love they have for her and her older brother Ben, who was born to them.

Christy Haines applauded the way her agency prepared her and husband Paul for adopting two teen-age girls who were from troubled homes. The Haines had to go through an intensive training program to become eligible to be an adoptive family; part of that training included a briefing on the girls' backgrounds. Christy said about her fourteen-year-old adopted daughter Stephanie, "The fact that I know she came from a family where some were not even high school graduates helps me to have more realistic expectations about her educationally. It keeps me from getting frustrated with her when she seems less than motivated to learn."

The parenting skills provided for their special-needs children are lauded by Gus and Letitia Reyes, who adopted brothers Tony and Ray through a state agency. The Reyes say the state helped prepare the boys for their "growing-up home," as the state termed the Reyes' home to them before the boys moved there. Workers encouraged the Reyes to make a video introducing the

> *"I believe it is an inherent trait in the human race. The more they can know, the more emotionally happy they will be."*

boys to the Reyes' house and required them to take a thirteen-week course helping prepare Gus and Letitia for the boys' reactions to things—even down to the way an unfamiliar house smells and unfamiliar bed linens feel.

The Reyes were grateful for the information the state provided them about the boys' original home even though the information was not all flattering. One of their sons seemed relieved that the Reyes spoke of his birth mother by name. "We have pictures of her. We don't want to make more of it or less of it than it is. It is a reality. But we're working on bonding with our family now," said Letitia. The Reyes say they will prepare the boys to meet their birth parents when the boys are adults. Said Gus of that prospect, "It's going to be tough. These parents made bad choices. The way we prepare them [to meet birth parents] is to help them have a solid understanding who they are in Christ. Christian parents help the child understand that 'I'm new in Christ. That's the stock I come from.' Then whatever they run into won't matter," he says.

Ready When Children Ask

Other parents, by networking, are finding out ways to take matters in their own hands to make adoption go successfully. Janice Duffy, who adopted six-year-old Andrea, and three-year-old Katie from Romania, say parents who adopt internationally can't always rely on those facilitating foreign adoption to get the background information they need. When she visited Romania to adopt Katie, Janice prevailed until she tracked down Katie's birth mother, who was living in extreme poverty and who had put all her children in an orphanage at birth. At that time Janice got basic information, such as name, age, health data. But when Janice's husband Roger returned to Romania sometime later to bring back Andrea, Katie's birth sister, he had dinner and breakfast with their birth mother and took along a good translator so he could query her at length for more details. "One of her grandfathers turned out to have been a neurosurgeon in Israel. If I hadn't known this, one day when Katie asks about her parents, I might have said, 'They were just country folks.' Now I can tell her more than that. I also found out that the birth father's father was a medical doctor. I feel that any person, no matter how happily they were reared, may have that need to know. I believe it's an inherent trait in the human race. The more they can know, the more emotionally happy they will be."

She encourages people who adopt internationally to dig immediately for as much background information as they can get while they're still in the foreign country. "Try to find out even if you think that you don't want to know," said Janice. "That child may turn sixteen and it may be the most important information in her life. People in these countries are poor and have little health care. The birth mother might not be alive then. If you think that you can later just write and find out information, you're wrong. It's too difficult."

Another of DePelchin's post-adoptive services is a seminar for adoptive parents who have wondered how they will feel if their child wants to meet his or her birth parents. Guests who attend hear from parents who have had this experience. The agency also holds a search workshop—not to dwell on how-tos but to explore the implications, feelings, and questions about contact. The seminar is for all parties in the adoption triad as well as birth and adoptive siblings, spouses, and friends.

Openness Too Late

But some of this openness has come too late for many people—persons like myself who were adopted thirty and forty years ago and who have little information and birth parents of that era who felt they were offered little support. For them there are agencies like ALMA, where members see themselves as a triangle with each side trying to support and understand the other. Mutual registries, enabling birth families and adopted individuals to know each other's whereabouts if both parties have registered, now exist in thirty-five states.[9] Seeing one's own records or original birth certificate without undertaking a cumbersome court or bureaucratic procedure now is possible only in Alaska, Hawaii, and Kansas.[10]

For example, Norma Tillman, a licensed private investigator in Tennessee who says she has found more than one thousand missing persons, lobbied to get the age for petitioning the state for identifying information lowered to age twenty-one, with the state conducting the search. As a result of delays, however, many hundreds of people still wait for searches, which cost the searching person. Tillman says her services are in such demand by parties in the adoption triad that she only conducts searches now if the person searching has the full correct name of the person sought, date of birth, and many specific identifiers. However, Tillman has a computer registry that matches people merely by furnishing facts such as date of birth, hospital, or agency. She also refers them to support groups like ALMA, which help people with searches; to a book by Jayne Askin, which tells laws of every state (see appendix C); and to her own book, *How to Find Almost Anyone, Anywhere.*

Some agencies like DePelchin are developing elaborate systems to help individuals search, with the agency facilitating the contact if it makes a connection. To help searching individuals from its agency, DePelchin has a computer program that Franzmeier describes as "perfectly legal" and that has access to a large data base. Franzmeier says some local judges will allow adoptees to obtain their birth information from court records "as long as they work through us" as facilitators. She says her agency will facilitate and mediate for adopted persons placed by other agencies as long as they have their own information and don't need DePelchin to search.

> *"Nowhere else in life besides adoption do we expect people to totally disconnect from their previous families."*

Agencies also encourage birth mothers who made adoption plans years ago to return for counseling even though they made their adoption plans in an entirely different era of adoption practices. Carolyn Wells, who directs the pregnancy/parenting/adolescent program for Volunteers of America in Louisiana, said, "One of the most difficult things to deal with is a birth mother who made an adoption plan thirty or forty years ago. [Those] birth mothers have never had permission to talk about this. I see a lot of depression in these people."

Curious Despite Information

People speculate that children won't want to search if they have grown up all of their lives with a wealth of background information, but there is no evidence to support such a view. Eight-year-old Margaret Mary Hays has a wealth of information about herself but says about her birth mother, "I'm still curious. I have a description of what she looks like, but I'd like to know what her feelings were and how she felt when she had to give me to a children's home and how she felt about giving me away."

DePelchin uses birth parents as resources for adoptive families when a child may need to meet or talk to a birth parent to get his or her questions satisfied.

"Nowhere else in life besides adoption do we expect people to totally disconnect from their previous families," said Franzmeier. She said that in one extreme case, she even helped arrange for a teen-age girl to go on a vacation with her birth mother, with her adopted parents' permission, when the teen-ager was determined that she might be happier with her birth family. "That child since then has spent several weeks each year with her birth family. She sees that she doesn't fit with them and that she's much better off with her adoptive family," said Franzmeier.

Just How Effective?

Developments such as open adoption and widely publicized cases in which birth parents have reneged on their decision and gone to court to reclaim children have caused people to raise issues about whether adoption is now too fraught with difficulty to be effective. As a result agencies are looking more carefully at the pre-placement process to make sure birth mothers study all sides of the issue—getting them to talk with birth mothers who choose to parent as well as those who made adoption plans. "They never realize how difficult [giving up that child] it will be," said Ivey. Bethany encourages clients to write their thoughts down in a workbook so that if a birth mother changes her mind about adoption and decides she wants to parent her child, caseworkers can help her look back at her workbook and track whether circumstances changed since the time she chose adoption.

As a result agencies are reaching out to birth fathers more—to try to locate them, to give them counseling, and to help them understand that it's okay to think about their children. When birth parents do change their minds and want to reclaim the child, agencies work to deal promptly with the situation, involving all individuals and negotiating honestly. This avoids the kind of lengthy trauma that parties in some recent, well-publicized cases had to go through. Agencies also urge states to have laws that insist on professional counseling of birth mothers before termination of their parental rights.[11]

States have post-adoptive services that are helping to spot problem adoptions before the adoption fails. For example, in New Jersey, which is considered one of the most progressive states in this area, a therapist is sent to adoptive homes for crisis counseling. If someone is about to adopt a child from a state agency in New Jersey, the prospective adoptive family members have to volunteer at the state agency for six months to observe the child's behavior and how the staff interacts with him or her. Parents waiting to adopt have to get involved with counseling services right away. [12]

Franzmeier says when adoptions disrupt, DePelchin now will consider looking back at the birth parents as potential adoptive parents rather than putting the child with someone totally nonconnected. "Sometimes [birth parents'] situations are different and they can rear this child now," she says.

Families Thriving

Although problem adoptions get much spotlight, successful adoption still is the norm, experts say. Fewer than 10 percent of the fifty thousand nonrelative adoptions in the USA each year are contested. Court fights are "unusual and not at all reflective of most of the adoptions that occur in the United States," says Howard Davidson, director of the American Bar Association Center on Children and Law.[13] Plenty of adoptive families are thriving, says Joe Kroll, executive director of the North American Council on Adoptable Children in Minneapolis. "If you've got good people with a commitment to parenting, and they've got a good support system to turn to, they're going to do a good job. I know plenty of birth kids who have given their parents a giant load of trouble, too. Sometimes even in the same family you see two adopted kids, one doing poorly and the other great."[14] Parent support groups can help adoptive families who aren't having any problems but who want to prevent them.

Clearly the concerns about adoption are not enough to turn off the one to two million parents who are trying to adopt. But 60 percent of the 160,000 or so children adopted every year in the U.S. are adopted by relatives or step-parents, leaving a small portion available for others.[15] Prospective parents usually have to wait at least two years to adopt.[16] This is a marked change from the 1950s, when an equilibrium existed between the number of infants needing families and couples who wanted to adopt.[17] From a high of 89,000 in 1970, nonrelative adoptions dwindled as birth control and abortion became more available and as single parenthood gained greater acceptance.[18]

Today just 2 percent of all abortions are for saving the life of the mother, mainly because of uterine cancer or ectopic pregnancies or for rape or incest, says Sylvia Boothe, coordinator for the Southern Baptist Home Mission Board's Alternatives to Abortion Ministries. Its purpose is to "educate, motivate, and equip Southern Baptists to become involved in long-term, positive ministry to those involved in crisis pregnancies.[19] Only 25,000 infants are placed for adoption every year, while 1.6 million are aborted. More than 1 million teenage girls—one in every ten under age twenty, become pregnant in the U.S. every year. Teens have 25 percent of all abortions.[20]

The reality of post-abortion syndrome (PAS) counters individuals who say they chose abortion over adoption because they did not believe they could live with the lifetime pain of separating from a birth child by making an adoption plan. Post-abortion syndrome, an adverse emotional or physical reaction to an abortion procedure occurring immediately or over a long period of time, has such symptoms as nightmares and recurrent dreams, flashback episodes, difficulty concentrating, depression, and anxiety. During the last decade dozens of post-abortion therapy and help organizations have sprung up among post-abortive women. Research is continuing to gather data on the extent of psychological harm abortion causes. [21] Groups are formed to counsel these persons as well.

Volunteering Homes and Help

A growing number of individuals volunteer their homes to be shepherding homes to house pregnant women who for various reasons need to be away from their family environment during their pregnancies. One such person, Jean Haworth of Ada, Oklahoma, who has housed about twenty young women during more than four years, says she began receiving women from homeless shelters, Salvation Army, and crisis pregnancy centers in her area just by getting the word out that she was available. "We just take them in and love them for who they are," she said. She says she usually goes to the hospital with them and stays with the women through delivery.

"Many times there's been a disruption with parents, but I've seen lots of restorations between girls and their mothers because they've had a chance to get away," she said. "One had been sleeping in a car before she came to us." Jean says she and her husband request that the women attend church with them, and none has protested. "It's brought a new awareness in our church because of this ministry, and the girls have had the opportunity to learn about God's love." Jean said she became involved in the project because she wanted to do something about abortion besides merely crusade.

Some friends expressed concern that the presence of the single mothers might wrongfully influence Jean's teen-age daughter, but Jean says her daughter has been an asset to the ministry. "She is a real friend to them," Jean says. "She doesn't want any part of this life. It has absolutely the opposite effect than what most people would think."

Juanette Jones, who formed a Memphis organization to help young women with crisis pregnancies after her own life was spared in a serious traffic accident, offers these tips for people who want to support women who elect not to abort their babies:

- Take dinners to a family providing a home to an unwed mother

- Pass on your unique gifts to young women in a crisis pregnancy (ceramics, cross-stitching, piano lessons, childbirth instruction, aerobics, nutrition, tutoring)

- Help young women in a maternity or foster home feel welcome by taking gifts or goodies

- Be a labor coach for a single pregnant woman

- Volunteer for crisis pregnancy counseling.[22]

Adopting Privately

Private adoptions, which some say are a humane way to end long waits for placement, are on the upswing. Sometimes these begin with a few hopeful lines in classified sections of newspapers. Although no statistics are available, specialists say private adoption now account for at least half of the twenty-five or more infant adoptions in the country each year. Private adoptions are closely regulated by courts, with requirements for pay, and adoptive parents must submit to a home study in which a social worker assesses the family's background and environment, with little difference in costs between private and agency adoptions.

Traditionally agencies say they are more equipped than are attorneys to manage adoption since they have decades of experience and expertise to assist birth mothers and adoptive parents, even years later. While an agency might be in existence thirty years later when an adoptee would search, an attorney might have disbanded practice, with no records available. However, for some the advantage is that in private adoptions, the trend is toward full disclosure, with adoptive couples and birth mother fully communicating with each other, so that most information is known at the time of placement.[23] Bethany's Sandy Ivey says many who adopted privately call her wanting to tap into agency helps which would go beyond the scope that an attorney could provide. "They're calling up saying, I know I didn't adopt with you, but my child is five; he's started to ask questions. What am I supposed to do?" she says.

Overseas adoptions also are on the increase, as couples hope to avoid failed adoptions and long waits. A 1993 report by the congressional General Accounting Office said international adoptions increased 10 percent the past year because those Americans surveyed didn't trust the permanency of adopting in the U.S. In 1992, 9,008 foreign children were adopted, compared to 7,093 in 1990. Most are from Romania and South Korea. At Small World adoption agency in Hermitage, Tennessee, the average cost is $8,000 to $12,000 including everything but plane fare. Foreign governments strictly regulate foreign adoptions. Foreign children are closely scrutinized by U.S. Immigration and Naturalization Service; health and background are checked.[24]

Another aspect that has helped adoption build a better mousetrap is a health-coverage break for adoptive parents. A federal benefits law now requires employers to treat adopted children the same as biological offspring in terms of medical coverage. Under the new law, an adopted child must be insured, regardless of pre-existing ailments, as soon as adoptive parents begin supporting the child.[25]

Getting on with Life

Open adoption, while on the surface appearing to be the answer to everyone's concerns about adoption and secrecy, is not without its critics. In open adoption ideally a child would be reared in an adoptive home clearly acknowledging his adoptive parents but without denying the other parents' existence or their importance. However, critics say that the birth mother will have a more difficult time getting on with her life if the ties are not severed permanently. They say that adoptive parents will feel they are merely caretakers rather than parents.

Instead of holding birth parents back from getting on with their lives, those involved in the process find that through open adoption the birth mother can grieve the loss more easily, if she sees that the child is in a good home.

Brian Fellers describes Brooke's birth mother's first visit with him and his wife Beth after Brooke was born: "We were nervous at first. I wasn't nervous for myself. The last time [we met] the baby was hers, and I wondered how it would make her feel. But Brooke went right to her. It went well. We understood that she [Brooke's birth mother] did a lot better [in her adjustment] after the first visit."

As for future contact, "We'll play it by ear," said Beth. "We'll make sure we send photos. I feel like from about age two until Brooke is an older teen, it would be better if she didn't see her." Said Beth about Brooke's birth mother, "She's like a part of our family. It's all based on trust."

People have feared that too much openness would totally derail adoption, provoking "an epidemic of teenagers knocking on birth parents' doors at midnight," but in England, Scotland, and Wales, where adoption records are totally open, fewer than 2 percent of adoptees have actually tracked down their birth families.[26] Other fears are that too much openness would lead birth mothers to try to reenter their child's lives. But statistics have held that only a small percentage of birth mothers actually undertake a search. Although 82 percent of birth mothers interviewed for a study said they would be comfortable with a reunion should their son or daughter desire it, only 5 percent were at that point searching for children.[27] Only about one hundred adoptees and some birth mothers request her agency's help in a search each year, despite the hundreds of children placed during the Houston agency's one hundred-year history, says Franzmeier.

Carla Monroe says her agency asks adoptive couples to write and send photos to the birth mother at one, three, six, nine, and twelve months. She says: "This is during the time of the baby's biggest change and a time when the birth mothers grieve more. Couples who send these generally care about her questions and concerns. We have a few where the birth mother meets the parents around the child's first birthday, some around the second birthday, and a few at school age when the child is fully aware that this is the birth mother. Most of the time it's strictly correspondence versus meeting. Couples are more comfortable doing this when their children are young rather than when they're older, when the child might feel a conflict of loyalties. Birth mothers do become upset if adoptive parents promise and don't correspond. We urge adoptive parents: Don't make promises to her that you can't keep." Sandy Ivey says her agency also notes that interest on the birth mother's part begins to taper off after the first year as their lives take on new focus.

"We get as much information as we can during pregnancy, because after they leave our care, we have no guarantees," said Monroe. "We ask adoptive parents to prepare a photo album, and we also ask birth mothers to give pictures of themselves. When children start to ask questions, parents then can say to children, 'Let's look,' and can turn to the album."

From the time of the first home studies agencies now emphasize the importance of biological roots and help parents understand that questions are normal. As a result of this educational process, "The majority of our adoptive families eagerly await that moment of being reunited with the birth mother. We run into very few that still feel threatened," says Ivey.

Says Monroe, "We are willing to help adoptees who come back. We go back to the birth mother's last-known address and see if we can track her down. We are the mediator. Most [birth parents] are absolutely thrilled. Very few say no. It's been very positive."

Using This Chapter

All parties in the adoption triad can benefit from becoming aware of the ways that the changing face of adoption applies to their particular situation.

☘ Avoid clinging to some misperception about adoption based on an archaic stereotype. Adoption practices are changing rapidly; something that seemed to be an impediment a year ago may have a totally new look today.

☘ Seek the help for birth relatives, adopted persons, and adoptive parents now available. If you've already connected with an agency or adoption-related group, find out how your needs can be met; if not, contact a reputable organization in your area or look in the appendix of this book for listings of places to write or call or materials to read that will demonstrate how adoption truly has built a better mousetrap.

T E N

The Blessings: A Goodly Heritage

The elderly man had lain comatose for days. Family members and friends had taken turns at his bedside as they tried in vain to rouse him. The devastation of four years of Alzheimer's disease, combined with this latest onslaught of a diabetic coma, pneumonia, and kidney failure, had taken their toll. The once robust frame now was gaunt; the once animated face was ravaged and thin.

With afternoon visiting hours, fresh company came, but the woman in the pair of new visitors didn't stop at the foot of the bed to survey the patient's status before she approached him. These guests had driven many miles to arrive at this moment, and the woman, fearing that spending time on formalities might cause her to be too late for her task, stepped up determinedly to bend near the patient's ear. Touching his frail hand, she addressed him as boldly as though he were waiting to carry on a full conversation. "Thank you," she whispered to the wizened, motionless head. Her simple act communicated more than words could: "Thank you for taking good care of my child and for making it possible for me to have a good life."

Only when I reach the other side of eternity will I know for sure whether Daddy was aware of Eleanor's visit with him in that Dallas hospital room during his final days on earth. He never stirred and never gave any outward sign to indicate that her words penetrated the deep coma from which he slipped several days later when his long life of eighty-eight years ended.

Yet the significance of that visit, when members of my two families were together in such a tender time in that hospital room, was one that surely must have made the bells of Heaven ring. It seemed that with that visit to his bedside, the events that began in another Dallas hospital more than four decades before as the doctor handed a woman's newborn baby to a special adoptive couple had come around full circle at last. This meeting seemed to give my birth mother the opportunity to put closure on and bring healing to some past events in her life and to feel at peace about the way God had used them for the good.

The special relationship between my parents and Charles and Eleanor during the years that they had known each other was one of the most joyous and rewarding results of the search and reunion process. On two different occasions, as they motored through Texas on one of their many post-retirement trips in their travel trailer, Charles and Eleanor had swung by to visit my parents at their home.

I can't imagine how heavy the steps of a birth mother must be as she walks through the rooms of someone else's house with walls literally papered in photos of a child that she carried in her womb yet didn't rear—photos that literally scream her name because of the physical resemblances that she sees. I cannot imagine how the heart of an adoptive mother must race as her thoughts fly back through years of diapers and piano recitals and prom dates and she realizes that all those precious mother/child experiences easily could have belonged to the person she is escorting instead of her. I can't imagine how my two mothers—so very different and yet so much a part of me—managed to make it through some of those gripping and highly personal moments.

Yet I know that somehow, these two families managed to carry these meetings off with as much grace and dignity as can be managed in such a potentially awkward situation. As I had envisioned, Daddy gave Charles a tour of the print shop that he operated in his garage during the years after he retired from his post-office career. He sent Charles home with a big sack of pecans that he picked from his pride-and-joy Texas pecan trees in his back yard. Eleanor spoke so fondly of the lemon bar cookies that my mother served during their first visit that my mother passed on the recipe to her. The two families for at least a decade exchanged Christmas greetings, with Charles and Eleanor reporting in their Christmas newsletter about their journeys to visit with the Wheeler family in Texas.

> *I saw that in God's good timing, things would work out in a far more significant way than I ever could have written the script for.*

Little deep conversation occurred during those moments, but the two families grew comfortable with each other, and it set the stage for the deeper exchange that would come years later. And although I originally chafed at not being present at those early meetings, I came to look on those times with profound gratitude for the great and almost magical connection that they provided between my two families for future years. And I saw that in God's good timing, things would work out in a far more significant way than I ever could have written the script for.

When time arrived for us to lay my dad's earthly body to rest and to celebrate his passage into eternal life, it surprised absolutely no one when my mother approached Charles and

Eleanor, who made a special trip to Garland for his funeral services, and said to them, "I want you to sit with our family when we go to the church tomorrow. I want you to come and be one of us."

Many report becoming more decisve, more outgoing, more determined in other areas of their lives as a result of understanding this venture.

As I turned back to look at this blended gathering assembled on five rows of family pews at the church that day, I was reminded again of a Scripture that had leaped off the pages of the Bible during my early search and reunion days. Once again, Psalm 16:6 came to mind, and I felt I truly could say, as the psalmist did, "The lines are fallen unto me in pleasant places; yea, I have a goodly heritage." And I was thankful that both streams of that goodly heritage could flow together on that day when we commemorated my father's homegoing to be with his heavenly Father.

Other adoptees negotiate for various degrees of openness with their adoptive family.

Tana Hill says one of her biggest challenges is telling her mother about times when she plans a visit to her birth family. "She is a tenderhearted woman, so I don't always broadcast it," said Tana. "But she certainly knows where I stand with her. Sometimes she is a little jealous, but she certainly realizes that she benefited the most."

Jacqueline Jagger says she lets her adoptive parents take the lead in asking her questions about contact with her birth family. After nine years in a relationship with her birth mother, Jacqueline believes that she and her parents have settled into a fairly comfortable pattern about when and how often to discuss this issue in her life so that her adoptive parents do not feel as if they are being dislodged.

Betsy DeShano says the whole experience has brought her and her mother closer together (her adoptive father died just before she began her search). She said the experience of walking through the fire to find her birth family, even with the adverse conditions that she learned about, has given her added confidence in her abilities—a self-esteem-building kind of experience that many other adoptees have noted also. Many report becoming more decisive, more outgoing, more determined in other areas of their lives as a result of undertaking this venture—a sort of "If-I-can-do-this-I-can-do-anything" mentality. In turn, the situation has added to her adoptive mother's confidence level because she feels assured she did the right thing in turning Betsy loose to search. As a result, the two women have developed an added appreciation and acceptance of each other. "We hug each other a lot more now," Betsy said. She said her adoptive mother "has pictures of my [birth] sisters on her 'family wall,'" and her sisters were attendants in her wedding when Betsy recently remarried.

Explaining to Another Generation

Another rewarding spinoff of my search and reunion was the joy of passing the story on to another generation, as Louis and I explained to our children how they acquired an extra set of grandparents and helped them understand this important part of their heritage. Because Matthew was three when I found my birth family, he grew up knowing the story—told to him in the same age-appropriate, manageable chunks that parents are advised to do when they're dealing with a child's sex education. We worked the words "birth mother" and "birth family" into his vocabulary in the same way my parents had worked the word "adopted" into mine.

As I would leave for my early trips to Denver, I would tell Matthew that I was going to visit my first mother—the one who carried me in her tummy but couldn't rear me, so she gave me to Grandma and Granddaddy to rear. And, as Matthew grew and the expected "Why not?" questions arose, I explained that Eleanor didn't have a husband and didn't have a job and that a helpful doctor, who knew Grandma and Granddaddy wanted a baby, made an adoption plan for me. We always tried to present any facts nonjudgmentally, because a strong bond developed between Matthew and Charles and Eleanor, and we wanted nothing to stand in the way of that relationship. He had been their first grandchild, and as he grew, they invited him to spend weeks with them in Colorado during the summer.

When Katie came along, we approached my adoption story with her in the same way, except that by the time she was born we had known my birth family for several years. From the start Katie knew she had three much-loved families of grandparents. A time never existed when they weren't a part of her frame of reference.

Reassurance about how grandchildren fit into the picture was a big concern for Wendy, Kristen Cunningham's birth mother, when she and Kristen visited in our home on one of Wendy's visits to Nashville. Kristen, Wendy, and Kristen's birth father, Donnie, and I had an enjoyable chat in which we compared notes about being adopted and listened to Wendy and Donnie share what it was like for them as birth parents to meet a beautiful and fully-grown daughter. Then my children entered the room for introductions. Suddenly the specter of relating to future grandchildren seemed to pop into Wendy's mind for the first time. Kristen and her husband Grant had no children yet, and the presence of Matthew and Katie prompted Wendy to think about a new set of issues.

"How do you explain a situation like this to children?" Wendy asked. I knew she was wondering how they would address the moral failure on the part of two individuals sensitively and without causing children to think less of their birth grandparents. I also assured her that the experience of grandchildren was one of the true joys of the adopted person-birth family reunion scenario. I assured her that Matthew and Katie thoroughly enjoyed their birth grandparents even though they from early childhood had known the story of how Eleanor and her family came to be part of all our lives. I told her how important it was to introduce our children to these facts promptly, matter-of-factly, and nonjudgmentally and to make sure we were always accessible should questions arise. Wendy seemed at ease as she considered the idea of someday relating to birth grandchildren.

Joe Wilson says he has taken his nine-year-old son and seven-year-old daughter to see both of their birth grandparents and wants to teach respect for them. "I ask them to call them 'Mr. Herman' and 'Miss Laverne.'" So far, Joe says he has tried to meet his children's level of curiosity with appropriate answers but says he will hold back no details when the time comes to tell about his abandonment. "I tend to be too judging about my mother and too easy on my father," he said. "But the truth was that they were both pretty young and naive. I think children can understand this."

Linda Sledge said the fact that some members of her birth family did not want to meet her and her family "was a good litmus test" of her sons' self-esteem. "The boys were astonished that they [her birth family] wouldn't want to meet them," she said. "They said, 'We're neat people. Why wouldn't they want to know us?' I believe this is a good mirror of how well you [as an adopted person] have dealt with it and accepted it yourself."

She said her sons took events in stride when she introduced to them a new set of kin—her uncle and aunt—and explained to her children how the families were related. "The reality for most families today is that their extended family lives far away," she said. "Introducing them to aunts, uncles, and cousins in their birth family is not much different from introducing someone to another branch of the family that they've never heard about."

A Fertile Ground to Teach

Although we tried to present the facts nonjudgmentally, we also tried never to shy away from the sex education aspects of my adoption story. We didn't want to glamorize it to the point that the children missed the critical issues of personal responsibility that the story clearly highlighted. Long before Matthew was a teenager, we used the story to illustrate the fact that personal decisions people make about their sexual behavior have serious and long-term consequences. A few moments in a motel room on the way to a movie or a prom may seem like a blip in history, but the consequences that result from those few moments can alter the course of people's lives forever. It can affect the way that they feel about themselves, about others, and about God. It can affect their economic stability, and it can affect the career choices that are available to them.

We also pointed out to Matthew that choices about sexual behavior continue to be vital when a person leaves the teenage years. Even people who are young adults—seemingly with their lives ahead of them—still have to be on guard about saying no to sex before they are married.

Linda Sledge said she also has used the story as a "huge dose of reality" for her two teenage sons. "Girls may not have as much difficulty envisioning the consequences in that they can see that they might have to rear the child, but it's often more difficult for boys." She said the entire scenario of finding her birth family has been for her sons "a moving picture of the consequences of one night."

We also emphasized the angle of vulnerability. Even if someone pledges to be sexually pure before marriage, weak moments can occur. It's sometimes difficult for teenagers who have high esteem to imagine that they ever could find themselves in a spot where their resolve could be tested, but a move to a new location, a job loss, the loss of a friendship, the lack of affection from a parent—all these can ravage people's self-worth to the point where they can be tempted to make wrong choices.

Matthew never balked at this part of the story. In fact, during his late adolescent years we were fortunate that the Southern Baptists' "True Love Waits" campaign encouraging sexual abstinence for teenagers strongly reinforced the message that he heard at home. Sometimes, however, he verbalized the contradictions. "But Mom, things turned out okay for everyone, didn't they?" he would ask. This was the difficult part. To him things did seem to have turned out okay: Eleanor had a successful career as a schoolteacher and wife and mother; my parents had the experience of being parents and grandparents; and I had a rich life full of appreciation for both heredity and environment. And when we all reunited in the end, we enjoyed knowing each other. To him, it meant more grandparents and therefore more attention. It was difficult at first for him to see anything potentially hurtful or devastating in anyone's life.

Although God helps us when we fall, He expects us to be on guard against stumbling in the first place.

We told him that our outcome was an example of God turning good out of a potentially harmful situation. As Romans 8:28 said, God truly did work all things together for good in this circumstance. God took care of all of us and brought all of us through a situation that could have been devastating. But we also told him that although God helps us when we fall, He expects us to be on guard against stumbling in the first place. We can't recreate the past and we can't erase history, but we can make sure we're obedient to Him in the future—and being obedient means following God's plan for sexual purity.

We have looked for teachable moments to reinforce this. Sometimes television talk shows, television sit-coms, and movies—with their contemporary themes of sexual promiscuity—make their way into our children's lives despite our best efforts to stop them. When this happens, we try to use these opportunities to interject this message to steer our children toward good choices.

"Whom We Wouldn't Have"

Even more profound has been the impact of my story to help teach my children about respect for life of the unborn. On a recent Sunday, bulletins in Southern Baptist churches throughout the United States featured Matthew's grinning face. The photo on the bulletin featured a nurse showing two teen-agers (one of them Matthew) a plastic model of a baby as it appears before birth. To me it was a splendid irony. The youth used in this theme photo to observe the Southern Baptists' Sanctity of Human Life Sunday—to help encourage women to choose life for their unborn babies—was the son of a child spared in the womb of an unmarried mother more than four decades earlier. It spoke to me about how God can use not only those of us who were given life but also the next generation of those who were given life to spread this all-important message—concern for the unborn.

> *God can use not only those of us who were given life but also the next generation of those who were given life to spread this all-important message—concern for the unborn.*

A highly dramatic moment in this area occurred when I and several others whose lives were affected by adoption participated in a panel discussion in front of a youth audience at our church. Two adult adoptees, an adoptive mother, and a teenager who had been adopted as a child spoke. As I and the others finished our testimonies, Matthew spoke up and told his fellow teenagers that he was thankful that my birth mother chose adoption, not abortion, because that decision also eventually meant life for himself and his sister.

Suddenly a male youth spoke up from the back of the room. "Wow, it's never dawned on me before now!" he exclaimed. "If we had had abortion, just look whom we wouldn't have. We wouldn't have Matthew, we wouldn't have Katie, we wouldn't have . . . ." and he went on to name numerous other of his adopted friends who clearly were dear to his heart. The roomful of teenagers was hushed for several minutes after that. Scotty had just brought the issue of abortion into some very practical terms for the youth in that room to think about. I was thankful for the word from Matthew that reflected on his own goodly heritage and helped give his own generation a tangible warning about abortion's destruction.

I was thankful for the word from Matthew that reflected on his own goodly heritage and helped give his own generation a tangible warning about abortion's destruction.

Another teenager whose very presence has been a visible example to other teens of life spared from abortion is Heidi Huffman of Spartanburg, South Carolina, who makes public stands highlighting the fact that she almost was an abortion statistic. Heidi makes speeches before rallies and retreats about how her mother, Tina, had a failed abortion when she was pregnant with Heidi. Later, after she carried Heidi safely to term, Tina became a Christian and active in urging other young women to avoid abortion's tragedy. As Heidi entered her teens, she joined her mother in her cause and has prompted many teenagers to think twice about aborting their babies as she boldly delivers the message, "My mom tried to abort me, but God said no. Thanks be to Him that I'm living." When asked how she—as a teenager—likes being thrust into the "very adult world of abortion," Heidi responds, "I don't think it's an adult issue, because there are girls thirteen and fourteen having abortions. This concerns anybody who is living."[1]

Opportunities for Ministry

My search and reunion story also opened tremendous ministry avenues for me. My story on adoption that the *Houston Chronicle* printed when I met my birth mother was for five years the newspaper's most frequently requested reprint. This indicated to me exactly how hungry people were for some guidance in dealing with their adoptive children on birth parent issues and how desperately many adoptees were to believe that their questions and curiosities were normal. I have spoken before audiences both secular and religious and before groups both large and small. Even though my story began to unfold many years ago, it always seems to fall afresh on the ears of parents who have just adopted, parents whose adoptive children have just begun to question, birth parents and grandparents whose pain of making an adoption plan for a child is recent and raw. I thank God for the opportunities I've had to use this story to minister to others, including some ways that were unexpected.

As a taxi once picked me up from a national conference where I spoke, I was counseling with a pastor who was an adoptive father and wanted to know how to share genetic information with his son. As the cab driver opened the door for me, I turned back to the father and promised him, "I will pray for you." Once inside the cab, the driver said he'd heard my parting comment to the man at the curb and questioned me about my faith. That conversation with the adoptive father paved the way for me to share with the cab driver about the Lord. All this occurred as an unplanned outgrowth of my adoption story.

Ministry opportunities also have occurred for my mother, as she's counseled with adoptive parents to encourage them to be open to their children's questions and to their searching for their birth families. At her church she volunteers with a program to counsel teen expectant moms. As she adjusted to life without my dad, the Lord has provided this new outlet for her to keep giving the gift of life to another generation as well.

Other adoptees find that the experience has plunged them heavily into working for adoption reform causes. Adult adoptee Richard Weizel is co-founder of Adoption Healing, a support group in Fairfield, Conn. He wrote, "My reunions have had such a profound impact on my life that I decided I couldn't sit and do nothing while so many others suffer because of the closed adoption system. I've come full circle, from an adoptee who didn't know if I even had the right to search, to an activist who won't rest until that right is secured for all."[2]

Peggy Dorn, a friend and inspiration in Houston who encouraged me in my search, has searched unsuccessfully for her birth family for years but did not let that deter her from helping other adoptees in her Orphan Voyage Organization. Jacqueline Jagger says she has counseled with adopted children, unwed pregnant teen-agers, and a friend whom Jacqueline was surprised to learn made an adoption plan for a child years ago. Marty Renault, whose meeting with her birth mother, Winnie, prompted my search after I interviewed them for the *Houston Chronicle*, remains active in ALMA and helps other adoptees with both the logistical and emotional aspects of their searches.

Carolyn Wells directs a post-adoption services unit for an adoption agency and speaks from personal as well as professional experience when adoptees and adoptive families seek her counsel on search-related issues.

Covered with Love

The search and reunion with my birth family also profoundly affected my own Christian testimony. As the words of Psalm 139 took on added significance for me, I realized that these words also represented a gift that kept on giving. Not only did God cover me with love from day one—during those days when I was being made in secret and was too tiny to even help myself—He was *still* covering me with love. Not only had He not dropped me then, from the very first moment a Kay existed, He had not dropped me since then either—not during times when doors were closed in front of me, when I had to settle for second best, or when other crises had occurred in my life. And as succeeding disappointments have occurred, I've been able to use that "day one" reference point as a reminder to myself. "He didn't drop you *then* [at conception] or *then* [at birth] or *then* [at some other dark time in my life], and is He about to start now? No way. No way."

I believe that these verses in Psalm 139 represent a promise that He will cover others too—birth mothers who believe no hope exists, adoptive parents in their parenting task, and adopted persons trying to make sense of who they are. God knew us from the beginning, even when we were being made in secret, and He's not about to drop us now. I believe that adopted persons especially after searching passionately, can look back at their history with more objectivity and gratitude and more awareness than ever of God's provision for them during a time when they were too small to make decisions for themselves. At the outset of my search, I wondered if my Christian faith would make any difference in this unusual experience in my life that I was about to step into, and I found that it did a thousandfold.

Adopted persons also express gratitude for the sense of fulfillment a successful search and reunion brings. "I have a lot more settled feelings now that the gaps and holes are filled," said Marty Renault, who has had an enduring rela-

tionship with Winnie for sixteen years. "The quest has subsided, and I feel that now I can
explain some of my own actions and temperaments. I can
understand some of my reactions—I'm reacting the way
Winnie reacts to things."

> *"First you're crazy in love with the person, then you settle down and start finding out each others' flaws and start accepting them, and then it deepens and mellows out."*

She compares the stages of
her long and successful relationship with Winnie to the
stages of a successful marriage:
"First you're crazy in love with
the person, then you settle down and start finding out each
others' flaws and start accepting them, and then it deepens
and mellows out."

A Circle Fully Closed

I had said that Eleanor's visit to the Dallas hospital room
when my father was dying had brought things full circle from
the day more than four decades before when J. D. and Mable
Wheeler arrived at a Dallas hospital to become parents for
Eleanor's newborn child. But there was still one final, climactic moment to come when the circle closed completely. It
occurred at the cemetery, when the graveside portion of the
service had ended and Eleanor and Charles said their goodbyes to return home to Colorado.

Some weeks later, over that grave, the memorial park would
lay down a bronze marker bearing the inscription, "For other
foundation can no man lay than is laid, which is Jesus
Christ—1 Corinthians 3:11." We chose this verse for Daddy's
marker because it seemed to symbolize his life. He made all
of his decisions—whether to build a house, buy a car, plan a
trip—only after he was sure he had a firm foundation of
information on which to build. Most importantly, it testified

to my dad's Christian foundation because of his faith in God. During his service, Louis and the other minister who officiated referred to this Christian foundation, and that verse became the theme of his service.

But that inscription of 1 Corinthians 3:11 on his marker was highly significant as it related to my adoption pilgrimage as well. Fifteen years before his death, when a much-loved daughter came to him seeking his blessing as she looked for her birth family, he was able to say an unequivocal yes. He knew that he and my mother had laid a strong foundation of love in my life that nothing—not even the introduction of a whole new set of birth family members—could shake. He wouldn't realize it at the time, but with that unequivocal yes, soon to be publicized to a half-million readers in that cutting-edge era of adoption reform, he and my mother modeled a new openness that soon would sweep through archaic adoption practices and that would spur other adoptive parents to similar courage in decades to come.

> *He knew that he and my mother had laid a strong foundation of love in my life that nothing—not even the introduction of a whole new set of birth family members—could shake.*

At the funeral were my aunt, cousins, and numerous close friends who never had met Eleanor, and the funeral was not only a chance for Eleanor and Charles to pay their respects to my mother but also was a thrilling opportunity for these friends and family members to meet my birth family about which they had heard so much. As I introduced them to Eleanor, I could see each draw back a little as though to survey her eyes, her nose, her mouth—a stranger's face so like that of the one they'd known as family for more than forty years.

But it was my one and only first cousin who uttered those beautiful words that represented the climactic moment to this dramatic occasion. As the crowd thinned and my cousin grabbed Eleanor's hand for a final goodbye, she said to Eleanor, "Thank you. Thank you for giving us Kay." And at that grand and glorious moment, only a few steps away from where the ground was about to close over my father's casket, the circle at last was complete.

My only regret later was that I didn't look up. Somehow I think if I had, I would have seen my daddy's angelic presence hovering overhead. It was an event I do not think he would have missed.

Using This Chapter

Adopted Persons

❦ Use your experience as a launching pad to minister to others. Become involved in the movement to end abortion. Help a birth mother, either through shepherding homes or through other means (see list of suggestions in appendix A). Volunteer with an adoptees' organization like ALMA. Offer to share your experiences with anyone involved in some aspect of adoption.

❦ Use the experience to determine what you really want out of life. With the gaps of your birth history closed, what other goals can you tackle that also may have seemed formidable. Finding a birth family doesn't solve all problems, but it does help the adopted individual to target those problems and to give them some perspective. Build on your perseverance and grit that you demonstrated with this accomplishment.

Adoptive Parents

❧ If your child has been part of a search and reunion experience, serve as role models for newer adoptive parents who may have doubts about how they'll react to their child's questions.

❧ Seek opportunities to meet your child's birth parents after a search takes place. God will give you strength to make it through awkward moments. Speak freely of your appreciation for them as well as your apprehensions, if some exist. Recognize that the experience may be part of one of the most healing and freeing experiences in their lives. A comfortable relationship can result that can bring joy and support to both families, since all are unalterably connected as parties in the adoption triad.

Birth Parents

❧ Don't pass up the opportunity to meet your child's adoptive parents. The opportunities for healing will far outweigh the potential for pain. Communicate your fears and apprehensions, but also communicate your appreciation and relief that the child you carried and gave birth to was reared with love and care.

❧ Continue to remember that your self-worth is not based on something that happened to you in the past but on the unconditional love and acceptance of God—a message that's vital for adoptive parents and adopted individuals as well. A resource called *Search for Significance* LIFE® Support Group Series Edition (see appendix C) is ideal for individual or small-group study to help people understand that their self-worth is based on how God sees them, not on what others think about them or how they treat them. You, too, can use this experience as a confidence builder. Many birth parents find the experience so freeing that they return to church after many years' absence or come to know the Lord, if they haven't already invited Him into their lives. Listen to what the Lord is saying to you through this search and reunion experience.

The Reality
of Adoption

🌿

*T*he *adoption of a child addresses a* critical need in the lives
of three parties. It provides a home for a child whose future
might have been uncertain; it provides an answer for a family
that has a compelling desire to have an outlet for its love; and
it resolves an unplanned event for individuals who choose at
a particular time in their lives not to be parents.

But adoption is not an instant, one-time occurrence that
can be observed, neatly wrapped up, and relegated to the
annals of history. The effects of that adoption will linger
forever in the life of that adopted person—even when he or
she enters adulthood. It will affect the adoptive parents'
parenting decisions from the moment that child enters the
threshold of that adoptive family's door. It will color—either
consciously or unconsciously—every relationship the birth
mother and the birth father enter throughout the remainder
of life and the way they parent any children they eventually
rear. Anyone in the adoption triad who tries to deny adoption's ripple effect in his or her life courts serious difficulties.

Yet never in history has such a plethora of helps been available for people affected by adoption, and never has a time existed more supportive of people who choose the adoption route—either as a way to build a family or as a way to deal with integrity with an unexpected life event—or of those individuals who as children had the decision made for them.

Anyone in the adoption triad who tries to deny adoption's ripple effect in his or her life courts serious difficulties.

Sometimes contemporary television and movie scripts and talk shows take a dim view of adoption and paint it as a laborious, tricky, and heartbreaking option for individuals. They protray it as far too emotionally complicated for people who must make some of the decisions just mentioned. While some cases of difficulty occur, this book points out that heartbreaking adoptions clearly are not the norm. As a result of some isolated, highly visible situations, people unfairly blacken adoption as a choice. These people would benefit from setting aside these closed attitudes and instead seeing adoption as a social institution that has become much more enlightened during recent decades, with changes continuing as a deeper understanding of adoption occurs. In truth, adoption never has been a better choice.

People who help adoptive parents are working hard to envision what kind of aids parents will need throughout their lives to strengthen family life and to help them with their parenting task. Ongoing counseling, support groups, workshops, books, and resources exist to offer encouragement at every turn. New modes of adoption practices that provide whatever degree of openness parties wish are available. And couples wanting to adopt but disarmed by the seeming unavailability of adoptable children will find no shortage of ways to add children to their home if the family truly is resourceful, committed, and flexible. The fact that 20,000 babies are abandoned in hospitals each year and the fact that 442,000 children are in foster care negates any thought that adoptable children are in short supply.

Adopted individuals now come into their adoptive homes with albums; genetic, medical, and social background histories; and even letters and gifts from their birth families—links to their heredity that adopted persons of my era never could fathom. Agencies or individuals who help make adoption plans now recognize the significant role this information plays in one's psychological makeup and make valiant efforts to collect thorough histories during the time they have the birth parents in their care. Counselors who know the best ways of helping with these identity issues are available for adopted persons when they are school-aged, adolescent, or in various stages of adulthood. Adoptive parents enter adoption today more educated than ever before about how to deal with children's questions and about the normalcy of such questions. Helps exist for adopted individuals if and when they want contact with their birth families. Counselors can educate them on the most appropriate methods for such meetings and can help them approach such situations in a realistic and emotionally healthy way; and mutual consent registries and search helps are also available.

> *As a result of some isolated, highly visible situations, people unfairly blacken adoption as a choice.*

Birth parents now are given permission to grieve the loss of the child they could not parent and can receive lifelong, compassionate, professional help in the separation process and in moves toward emotional stability. Resources are available to help with the self-worth issues they feel in learning to forgive themselves and others and to help them resume life pursuits. Help also is available in later life as they adjust to the possibility of a reunion with the adopted person and possibly learn to relate to the child's adoptive family. Varying degrees of openness during the child's growing up years now can also be negotiated with the adoptive family, with the agency's help.

In truth, adoption has never been a better choice.

And for women at the time their pregnancy becomes apparent, crisis pregnancy centers exist—many through churches—to help persuade women to spare the lives of their unborn child. Shepherding homes provide a loving, caring environment while women who need to be away from their own residence wait out their pregnancies. Agencies are fine-tuning their counseling of birth parents to guard against any hint of pressure tactics and to include explanations of the grief process, which they believe will help adoption disruption later and keep parents from wanting to reclaim their child after relinquishment.

No one ever has promised that adoption will be struggle-free for any of the parties involved, just as no one can promise that any aspect of life will be free of twists and turns. But when those storms occur, more lifelines than ever are available to help the process.

If you believe in adoption, what can you do individually to keep it a strong and appealing choice? Demonstrate compassion by becoming personally involved with individuals experiencing unplanned pregnancies and offer personal involvement. Consider being a shepherding home or volunteering at a crisis pregnancy center or taking another of the actions described in appendix A to help individuals with unplanned pregnancies.

Push for openness. Speak out at churches and civic groups about your involvement in adoption and how you have seen it work. Get to know some adoptive families and see how their lives underscore or refute stereotypes about adoption. Are these families any different from other families you know in terms of their joys, struggles, challenges, milestones? Consider working on the public policy end for uniform adoption laws, open records, or ending long waits in foster care. Urge crisis pregnancy centers and other groups ministering to single, pregnant women to present adoption in a convincing manner. Read and be knowledgeable; go beyond the myths and get the facts for yourself. Then after you have obtained them, step in to correct gossip or misinformation about adoption wherever you encounter it.

Above all, be a ready ally to any of the parties involved in adoption.

Simply be available to listen, rejoice, cry, wait, and pray with them as they go through whatever pilgrimage confronts them. Adoption needs all the friends it can get.

N O T E S

Chapter One

1. Richard Weizel, "Is Blood Thicker than Adoption?" *USA Weekend*, March 20–22, 1992, 10.

2. T. S. Elliot, "Little Gidding," *The Complete Poems and Plays, 1909–1950* (New York: Harcourt Brace Jovanovich, 1952), 145.

Chapter Three

1. Richard Weizel, "Is Blood Thicker Than Adoption?", *USA Weekend*, March 20–22, 1992.

2. Susan Chira, "Years after Adoption, Adults Find Past, and New Hurdles," *The New York Times*, August 30, 1993, C–11.

Chapter Four

1. Arthur D. Sorosky; Annette Baran, and Reuben Pannor, *The Adoption Triangle* (Garden City, N.Y.: Anchor Press, 1978), 14.

Chapter Six

1. Bob Rose, "Adoption: The Other A Word," *Home Life*, April 1994, 39–41.

2. Elena Urumova, "Children Seek Their Roots: Adoption Search for Birth Parents Big Business," *The Tennessean*, September 26, 1993, 1B.

3. Karen M. Thomas, "New Family Ties," *Dallas Morning News*, July 24, 1993, 1C.

Chapter Seven

1. Susan Chira, "Years After Adoption, Adults Find Past, and New Hurdles," *The New York Times,* August 30, 1993, C–11.

2. Lorraine Dusky, "The Daughter I Gave Away," *Newsweek,* March 30, 1992, 12.

3. "Lynn Minton Reports: Fresh Voices—In Search of My Birth Mother" *Parade* Magazine, January 24, 1993, 16–17.

4. Dusky, "The Daughter I Gave Away."

Chapter Eight

1. Suzanne Arguello, "Ministering to Couples Who Are in the Adoption Process," *The Sunday School Leader:* Larger Church Edition, January 1994, 36–37.

Chapter Nine

1. Kathleen Silber and Phylis Speedlin, *Dear Birthmother* (San Antonio: Corona Publishing Co., 1983), 2–3.

2. W. Terry Whalin, "Living Out Her Books: Ann Kiemel Anderson," *The Christian Communicator,* November 1993, 2.

3. Stacey Freedenthal, "Adopted Children Visit Birth Parents at Hope Cottage Picnic," *Dallas Morning News,* June 8, 1992, 15A.

4. Michael Precker, "Adopting a New Attitude", *Dallas Morning News,* November 10, 1992, 5C.

5. Karen M. Thomas, "New Family Ties," *Dallas Morning News,* July 24, 1993, 1c.

6. Freedenthal, "Adopted Children Visit."

7. Ibid.

8. Mary Sue Kendrick, "Turbulent Teen Years Can Create Special Problems for Adopted Teens," *Bethany Review,* a publication of Bethany Christian Services, Fall 1993, 5.

9. Marilyn Elias, "How Adoption Echoes Through Family Life," *USA Today,* February 25, 1993, 6D.

10. Katharine Davis Fishman, "Problem Adoptions," *Atlantic Monthly*, September 1992, 50.

11. "Baby Jessica's Case Brings Mixed Feelings, Need for New Laws," *Bethany Review*, a publication of Bethany Christian Services, Fall 1993, 3.

12. Fishman, "Problem Adoptions," 69.

13. Desda Moss, "Tangled, Troubled Adoptions Spur Reform Call," *USA Today*, May 3, 1993, 9a.

14. Elias, "How Adoption Echoes."

15. Charlotte Allen, "Our Archaic Adoption Laws," *The Wall Street Journal*, August 11, 1993, A9.

16. Steven Waldman and Lincoln Caplan, "The Controversy Over Adoption," *The News Herald*, March 30, 1994, 18.

17. Janet Lynn Garey, "The History of Adoption, Or You've Come a Long Way, Baby," *The News Herald*, December 10, 1994, 1.

18. Moss, "Tangled, Troubled Adoptions."

19. Baptist Press, June 17, 1992.

20. Joseph P. Shapiro, "The Teen Pregnancy Boom," *U.S. News and World Report*, July 13, 1992.

21. "Tearing Down the Wall: Facing the Reality of Postabortion Syndrome," (pamphlet) Human Development Resource Council Inc., Norcross, GA, 1992.

22. "52 Simple Things You Can Do to be Pro–Life," (information sheet) Life Choices, Memphis, TN.

23. Kevin Sullivan, "Wanted: Baby for Loving Home," *The Washington Post*, October 5, 1992, A1.

24. Carrie Ferguson, "More Adults Look Overseas to Adopt,"*The Tennessean*, May 5, 1993, 1B.

25. Sue Shellenbarger, "Work & Family: Adoptive Parents Get Health–Coverage Break," *The Wall Street Journal*, September 3, 1993, B1.

26. Fishman, "Problem Adoptions," 50.

27. Sandra Evans, "The Other Side of Adoption," *The Washington Post*, January 16, 1994, 11.

Chapter Ten

1. "The Miracle Child," *Focus on the Family*, May 1993, 2–5.

2. Richard Weizel, "Is Blood Thicker Than Adoption?" *USA Weekend*, March 20–22, 1992

20 Simple Things You Can Do to Help Women Who Have Unplanned Pregnancies

1. Take dinners to a family providing a home to an expectant single mother.

2. Pass on your unique gifts to young women in a crisis pregnancy. Teach ceramics, cross-stitching, piano lessons, childbirth helps, aerobics, nutrition, tutoring.

3. Help make young women in a maternity or foster home feel welcome by taking gifts or goodies.

4. Give a party—cosmetics, kitchenware, toys, jewelry— and donate part of your proceeds to a ministry that helps expectant mothers with unplanned pregnancies.

5. Offer to drive young women in a maternity or foster home to worship at your church.

6. Give financially.

7. Be a labor coach for a single pregnant woman.

8. Mend/make clothing for this type of ministry.

9. Host a baby shower.

10. Shop garage sales and thrift stores for baby items and furniture to donate.

11. Become substitute houseparents of a maternity home or foster home.

12. Enhance self-image with a single pregnant woman. Study a book such as *Search for Significance* by Robert S. McGee with a pregnant woman or group of single expectant mothers during their pregnancies.

13. Walk or sponsor someone in a walk-a-thon or other fund-raising events such as tennis and golf tournaments to benefit a ministry to single pregnant women.

14. Be an extended family to a young woman in need.

15. Pray for ministries that encourage single pregnant women to give life to their unborn babies.

16. Offer to babysit for a single parent or the parents of a handicapped child.

17. Offer your professional services—construction work, contracting, auto mechanics, law, dentistry, medicine, printing, bookkeeping, accounting—to ministries that work with young women in crisis pregnancies.

18. Bake a treat for a ministry to young women with unplanned pregnancies.

19. Be a foster parent for an adoption agency.

20. Volunteer at your pregnancy counseling center—counseling, hot line, prayer line, receptions, or sort maternity and baby clothing.

—Adapted from suggestions by
Life Choices, Memphis, Tennessee

An Adoption Vocabulary

The language we use to describe adoption influences our attitudes and the feelings we have about birth parents, adoptive parents, and adopted individuals. The following are examples of terms recommended when speaking about adoption.

Instead of	Use
adoptee	adopted person, adult, child (use only if fact of adoption is important)
my/our child	birth child (only if fact of birth is important)
real parent	birth parent
natural parent/one's own parent	biological parent
unwed/unmarried mother	single mother
unwanted pregnancy/ out-of-wedlock pregnancy	woman with unplanned or crisis pregnancy
keeping the baby	parenting the baby
gave it away/give up a baby	make an adoption plan, planned adoption
surrendered/put up a child for adoption	transfer of parental rights
orphan/foreign child	child from abroad or another country

—*From "New Standards in Adoption Vocabulary,"*
Bethany Review (Fall 1991).

A P P E N D I X   C

Adoption Resources

Books/Booklets for Parties
in the Adoption Triad

Alexander-Roberts, Colleen. *The Essential Adoption Handbook* (Dallas: Taylor Publishing, 1993). Walks readers through the process step by step, covering all types of adoptions and the situations people may encounter. Samples of necessary letters, forms, and documents and how to present yourself as an adoptive parent.

Askin, Jayne, and Bob Oskam. *Search: A Handbook for Adoptees and Birth Parents* (New York: Harper & Row, 1982). A comprehensive how-to guide to searching for parties involved in the adoption process.

Bartholet, Elizabeth. *Family Bonds: Adoption and the Politics of Parenting* (Boston: Houghton Mifflin, 1993). Helps infertile couples consider adoption as a more desirable alternative than endless and expensive fertility procedures.

Boothe, Sylvia. *No Easy Choices: The Dilemma of Crisis Pregnancy* (Birmingham, Ala.: New Hope, 1990). Guidance and help for the concerned Christian who wants to minister to a woman with a crisis pregnancy.

Boothe, Sylvia. *Not an Easy Time: Help While You Are Pregnant* (Birmingham, Ala.: New Hope, 1990). Booklet helps individuals who are young, single, and having a baby and are trying to decide whether to marry, rear a child alone, or make an adoption plan.

Connelly, Maureen. *Given in Love: Releasing a Child for Adoption* (Omaha, Neb.: Centering Corporation, 1990). A compassionate booklet which helps birth mothers cope with the basic issues involved in the adoption choice. (Order from 402-553-1200.)

Gathering the Missing Pieces in an Adopted Life

Crain, Connie, and Janice Duffy. *How to Adopt: A Guide for Prospective Parents* (Nashville: Thomas Nelson, 1994). Answers the most frequently asked questions about adoption. Analyzes the various forms of adoption, such as international, state and special-needs, single-parent, agency, and private adoption.

Fisher, Florence. *The Search for Anna Fisher* (New York: Fawcett Crest Books, 1973). Landmark book that is the autobiographical account of the founder of ALMA's search to find her birth family.

Jewett, Claudia L. *Adopting the Older Child* (Harvard, Mass.: The Harvard Common Press, 1978). Explains the perils, joys, trials, and successes of older-child adoption and practical ways of dealing with these situations.

Kruzel, Pamela G. *Private Adoption: A Guide to Success* (Glenview, Ill.: P.K. Publications, 1993). Gives detailed information for developing an adoption plan. Booklet available by mail order from P.O. Box 2443, Glenview, IL, 60025.

Martin, Cynthia. *Beating the Adoption Game* (San Diego, Calif.: Harcourt Brace Jovanovich, 1988). Helps adoptive parents present themselves in the best manner possible and points out some abuses and red tape encountered by people wishing to adopt.

Melina, Lois Ruskai. *Raising Adopted Children: A Manual for Adoptive Parents* (New York: HarperPerennial, 1986). Draws on research to provide practical help, such as when and how to tell your child about adoption, what schools should know, adoption and adolescence, and how infertility affects roles as adoptive parents.

Melina, Lois Ruskai, and Sharon Kaplan Roszia. *The Open Adoption Experience* (New York: HarperPerennial, 1993). A complete guide for adoptive and birth families from making the open adoption decision through the child's early years.

Michelman, Stanley. *The Private Adoption Handbook* (New York: Villard Books, 1988). A step-by-step guide to the legal, emotional, and practical demands of adopting a baby through private adoption.

Posner, Julia. *The Adoption Resource Guide: A National Directory of Licensed Agencies* (Washington, D.C.: Child Welfare League of America, 1990). Offers a listing of public adoption programs in each state, private licensed agencies, national child welfare organizations, and search and reunion resources. Order from CWLA, c/o CSSC, P.O. Box 7816, 300 Raritan Center Parkway, Edison, NJ 08818.

Silber, Kathleen, and Phylis Speedlin. *Dear Birthmother: Thank You for Our Baby* (San Antonio: Corona Publishing, 1983). Shares letters exchanged between birth mothers and adoptive parents during the early days of open adoption.

Silber, Kathleen, and Patricia Martinez Dorner. *Children of Open Adoption* (San Antonio: Corona Publishing, 1990). A study of the first wave of children adopted through the open adoption process.

Rosenberg, Elinor. *The Adoption Life Cycle: The Children and Their Families Through the Years* (New York: The Free Press/MacMillian, 1993). How adoption can affect all parties involved across their life spans.

Sorosky, Arthur D, Annette Baran, and Reuben Pannor. *The Adoption Triangle* (Garden City, N.Y.: (Anchor Press/Doubleday, 1978). Studies the effects of the sealed adoption record on adoptees, birth parents, and adoptive parents.

Strom, Kay Marshall, and Douglas R. Donnelly. *The Complete Adoption Handbook* (Grand Rapids: Zondervan, 1992). Guides readers through the considerations and legalities that surround adoption to the final question: Is adoption for you? Covers special child adoptions, single parent adoptions, open and closed adoptions, unsuccessful adoption, international adoption, and explains state-by-state adoption policies.

Tillman, Norma. *How to Find Almost Anyone, Anywhere* (Nashville: Rutledge Hill Press, 1994). A collection of helps for people who seek to locate other individuals.

Wicks, Ben. *Yesterday They Took My Baby: True Stories of Adoption* (Toronto: Stoddart Publishing, 1993). A collection of oral histories of adopted persons, adoptive parents, and birth parents as they tell about how adoption has affected their lives.

Books for Children

Banish, Roslyn, with Jennifer Jordan-Wong. *A Forever Family* (New York: Harper Trophy, 1992). Eight-year-old Jennifer tells what it's like— after being a foster child in several different homes—to be adopted at last.

Fowler, Susie Gregg. *When Joel Comes Home* (New York: Greenwillow Books, 1993). A little girl describes all the things she and her parents are planning to welcome home friends and their newly adopted son.

Gathering the Missing Pieces in an Adopted Life

Girard, Linda Walvoord. *Adoption Is for Always* (Niles, Ill.: Albert Whitman & Co., 1986). Shows how Celia's adoptive parents forthrightly answer her questions about her birth family and accept her feelings when she initially reacts with insecurity about having been adopted. Includes factual information about the adoption process.

Krementz, Jill. *How It Feels to Be Adopted* (New York: Alfred A. Knopf, 1982). Nineteen children, ages 8–16, confide their feelings about all aspects of their adoption. Especially good reading for older adopted children.

Koehler, Phoebe. *The Day We Met You* (New York: Bradbury, 1990). A simple story that helps parents share the excitement of that important day with their adopted child.

Lifton, Betty Jean. *Tell Me a Real Adoption Story* (New York: Alfred A. Knopf, 1993). The story of an adopted child who asks questions and who wants to hear an authentic story. Story based on an adoption in which the adoptive parents meet the birth mother briefly. Parents can personalize for their own child.

Livingston, Carole. *Why Was I Adopted?* (New York: Lyle Stuart, 1990). A simple explanation for children of the facts of adoption.

Schnitter, Jane T. *William Is My Brother* (Indianapolis, Ind.: Perspectives Press, 1991) Family with two sons, one born into family, one adopted; explains the differences about how the two boys came to be brothers.

Wasson, Valentina P. *The Chosen Baby* (New York: HarperCollins Publishers: 1939, revised 1977). This classic children's story, first published in 1939, is newly illustrated and updated and communicates the joys adopted parents feel when a child comes into their home.

Musical Album

My Forever Family
Sweet Silver Enterprises
P.O. Box 120-493
Nashville, TN 37212

Two adoptive mothers' music expresses feelings of parents and adoptive children. Has adult side and children's side.

Abstinence Education

True Love Waits Campaign

An annual emphasis designed to be used in churches of all denominations to challenge teenagers and college students to remain sexually pure until marriage. It includes a series of Christian sex education resources for children, youth, and married couples. The resources include Boys and Girls—Alike and Different (ages 4–7); My Body and Me (ages 8–9); Sex! What's That? (ages 10–13); Sexuality: God's Gift (ages 14–17), and Celebrating Sex in Your Marriage (married couples). Order by calling 800-458-2772.

Support-Group Resources

Mcgee, Robert S. *Search for Significance* LIFE® Support Group Series Edition (Houston: Rapha, 1992). Helps individuals who struggle with low self-worth understand that the source of their self-worth is their identity in Christ, not others' approval or shame from past events.

Sledge, Tim. *Making Peace with Your Past* (Nashville: LifeWay Press, 1992). Helps people understand how painful events and issues in their past color their relationships to others in the present.

Sledge, Tim. *Moving Beyond Your Past* (Nashville, LifeWay Press, 1994). This sequel to *Making Peace with Your Past* helps individuals, with Christ's help, move beyond the hurts of the past and into joyful, productive day-to-day living.

Springle, Pat. *Untangling Relationships* (Houston: Rapha, 1993). Helps people understand how relationships become unhealthy and learn to develop Christ-honoring relationships with friends, spouses, children, co-workers, and others in their lives.

Springle, Pat. *Conquering Codependency: A Christ-Centered 12-Step Process* (Houston: Rapha, 1993). Helps people whose lives are devastated by codependency, the compulsion to rescue others and to control Utilizes a Christ-centered approach to the 12 Steps of Alcoholics Anonymous.

Adoption Organizations

Infertility

Resolve, Inc.
1310 Broadway
Summerville, MA 02144
617-623-0744

A nonprofit organization offering services to infertile couples. Chapters in all states and most cities. Local groups offer pre-adoption support groups, adoption information, and referrals.

Helps for Adoptive Families

Adoptive Families of America
3333 Highway 100 North
Minneapolis, MN 55422
612-535-4829 (24-hour helpline)

This nonprofit parent support organization provides information, education, and support to adoptive families, with 15,000 members worldwide. Their bimonthly magazine is *Adoptive Families* (formerly called *OURS*). They can provide a network of caring people willing to assist people with the same problems they have encountered.

National Adoption Information Clearinghouse (NAIC)
11426 Rockville Pike, Suite 410
Rockville, MD 20852
301-231-6512

Offers free literature for prospective parents as well as a file of adoption experts. Publishes a range of adoption materials including adoption directories, referrals to adoption experts, films and videotapes on adoption, and fact sheets on every aspect of adoption.

National Council for Adoption
1930 Seventeenth Street NW
Washington, DC 20009
National Adoption Hotline 202-328-8072

A nonprofit organization founded to strengthen adoption and related services, with a primary goal of promoting adoption as a positive option for young, single, or troubled parents. They publish the Adoption Factbook and some newsletters and provide coordination between national organizations and local service providers. Call their hotline for information and referral on maternity services, adoption resources, and infertility support groups in your area.

North American Council on Adoptable Children
970 Raymond Ave., Suite 106
St. Paul, MN 55114-1149
612-644-3036

A nonprofit coalition of parents, workers, and others committed to seeing that all special-needs children in the United States and Canada get permanent homes. Provides lists of local parents groups and provides models of post-adoptive services, technical assistance on subsidized adoption, and recruitment activities, especially for minority families.

Latin American Parents' Association
P.O. Box 523
Unionville, CT 06085-0523
203-270-1424

A network of families who help those seeking to adopt and who have adopted children from Latin America. Besides the organization in Connecticut listed above, other chapters exist in New York, New Jersey, and Maryland.

Over-40 Prospective Adoptive Parents

The Directory for Adoptive Parents Over 40
Adoption Resources & Communications
P.O. Box 509
Welcome, NC 27374
704-731-3348

A resource of helps for people over 40 who want to adopt. Lists groups and individuals who will work with older parents to find and adopt a child.

Appendix D

Special-Needs Children

AASK America
Adopt a Special Kid
2201 Broadway, Suite 702
Oakland, CA 94612
510 451 1748

Finds homes for children with special needs—minority children, disabled, too old to be adopted, or children who are neglected or abused.

Adoption Options
1724 N. Burnside, Suite 6
Gonzales, LA 70737
504-644-1033

Finds homes for hard-to-place children (mostly caucasian—those with birth defects, major or minor handicaps, at-risk babies, or those who are drug exposed).

Pro-Adoption Publications

Adoption Advocates NEWSLetter
1921 Ohio Street NE
Palm Bay, FL 32907
407-724-0815

Publishes monthly newsletter for people who are pro-adoption. Features latest developments in adoption practices.

Adoptive Families magazine (formerly *OURS*)
Adoptive Families of America
3333 Hwy. 100N
Minneapolis, MN 55422
612-535-4829

Published bimonthly, this magazine provides information on all aspects of adoptive parenting.

Organizations for Adopted Persons, Adoptive Parents, and Birth Parents

Adoptees Liberty Movement Association
P.O. Box 154
Washington Bridge Station
New York, New York 10033
212-581-1568

Provides information and support for persons affected by adoption. Provides search information and information on local groups nationwide.

American Adoption Congress
1000 Connecticut Ave., NW, Suite 9
Washington, DC 20036
202-483-3399

Nonprofit, international educational network dedicated to promoting openness and honesty in adoption. Conferences, national forum for search and support groups, helps in conducting searches for AAC members, and a newsletter that provides current trends in adoption movement.

Council for Equal Rights in Adoption
401 E. 74th Street
New York, NY 10021
212-988-0110

A network of 308 adoption search and support groups, adoption agencies, and mental health facilities in the United States and seven other countries.

Concerned United Birthparents
2000 Walker Street
Des Moines, IA 50317
1-800-822-2777

A national support and search organization for persons affected by adoption.

Appendix D

Searching for Lost Persons

International Soundex Reunion Registry
P.O. Box 2312
Carson City, NV 89702
702-882-7755

A nonprofit organization that operates a mutual consent registry, with no fees charged for people searching to register themselves.

People Searching News
P.O. Box 22611
Ft. Lauderdale, Florida 33325
305-370-7100

Newsletter with help for people who are searching for individuals. It provides information on reunion registries and has books and videos on post-adoption or search issues.

Reunions, The Magazine
P.O. Box 11727
Milwaukee, WI 52211
414-263-4567

A magazine featuring articles on adoptee-birth parent reunions as well as a classified section for those searching.

Unlimited Facts Obtained
Norma Tillman, Director
P.O. Box 290333
Nashville, TN 37029

This agency is representative of a number of individuals and agencies that conduct searches and help match parties of the adoption triad that may be seeking each other.

Pro-Life Helps
Alternatives to Abortion Ministries
Home Mission Board of the Southern Baptist Convention
1350 Spring Street, NW
Atlanta, GA 30367-5601
800-962-0851

Equips churches and individuals that want to start ministries to help those involved in crisis pregnancies. Maintains a nationwide database of crisis pregnancy centers to refer individuals calling the 800 number. Besides distributing *Not an Easy Time* and *No Easy Choices* (listed in appendix C) this ministry also provides the pamphlets, "What Is a Crisis Pregnancy Center?" "How to Establish a Crisis Pregnancy Center" and "Alternatives to Abortion Ministry."

> American Life League
> P.O. Box 1350
> Stafford, VA 22555
> 703-659-4171

Publication: *Celebrate Life*, a magazine featuring pro-life, pro-family issues. Also can provide information about the Huffmans mentioned in chapter 10, or a 24-minute video containing their story.

> Christian Life Commission of the
> Southern Baptist Convention
> 901 Commerce, #550
> Nashville, Tennessee 37203-3696
> 615-244-2495
> Pamphlets:
> "The Sanctity of Human Life: Abortion and the Law"
> "The Sanctity of Human Life: Alternatives to Abortion—Suggestions
> for Action"
> "Issues & Answers: Teenage Pregnancy"
> "Critical Issues: What the Bible Teaches About Abortion"
> "Critical Issues: Southern Baptist Heritage of Life"

> National Right to Life Committee
> 419 Seventh St, NW, Suite 500
> Washington, DC 20004

Publication: *NRL News*. Newsletter keeps people informed about the fight to save unborn babies, many of whom would be candidates for adoption.

> Life Choices
> 8608 Tree Court W.
> Memphis, TN 38018
> 901-756-5799

Provides crisis pregnancy counseling and post-abortion syndrome counseling.

Post-Abortion Syndrome

P. A.M. (Post-Abortion Ministries)
P.O. Box 3092
Landover Hills, MD 20784-0092
301-773-4630

Provides literature and outreach for men and women who have experienced abortion and want help with the resulting emotional and spiritual aftermath.

Christian Action Council
101 W. Broad Street, Suite 500
Falls Church, VA 22046
703-237-2100

Provides post-abortion counseling and education and counseling for women in crisis pregnancy. Produces, "The Action Line," a bimonthly newsletter, and other resources.

Kay's adoptive parents, J. D. and Mable Wheeler

Kay and
Catharine on
Catharine's
wedding day

Jean and Eleanor
late November, 1948

Kay, Louis, and Matthew—the family of three

Matthew's senior portrait

Eleanor's father

Kay with Mammaw
and Bandad

Charles, Eleanor, and their pets

Kay, Eleanor, and Catharine during Kay's
first visit to Colorado

Four generations

Catharine Louisa and her grandmothers

Matthew's high school graduation with his
grandparents

Eleanor as a school-
teacher in Colorado

Charles and Eleanor

Eleanor and Kay, Christmas, 1992